List of tourist attractions to color in this book

Eiffel Tower
Pisa Tower
Taj Mahal
Statue of Liberty
Statue oh Christ the Redeemer
Big Ben
Coliseum
Great Wall of China
Sidney Opera House
Chichén Itzá
Parthenon
Venice
Lombard Street
Golden Gate
Matterhorn and Alps
Pyramids of Giza
Louvre Museum
City of Ballons

PM

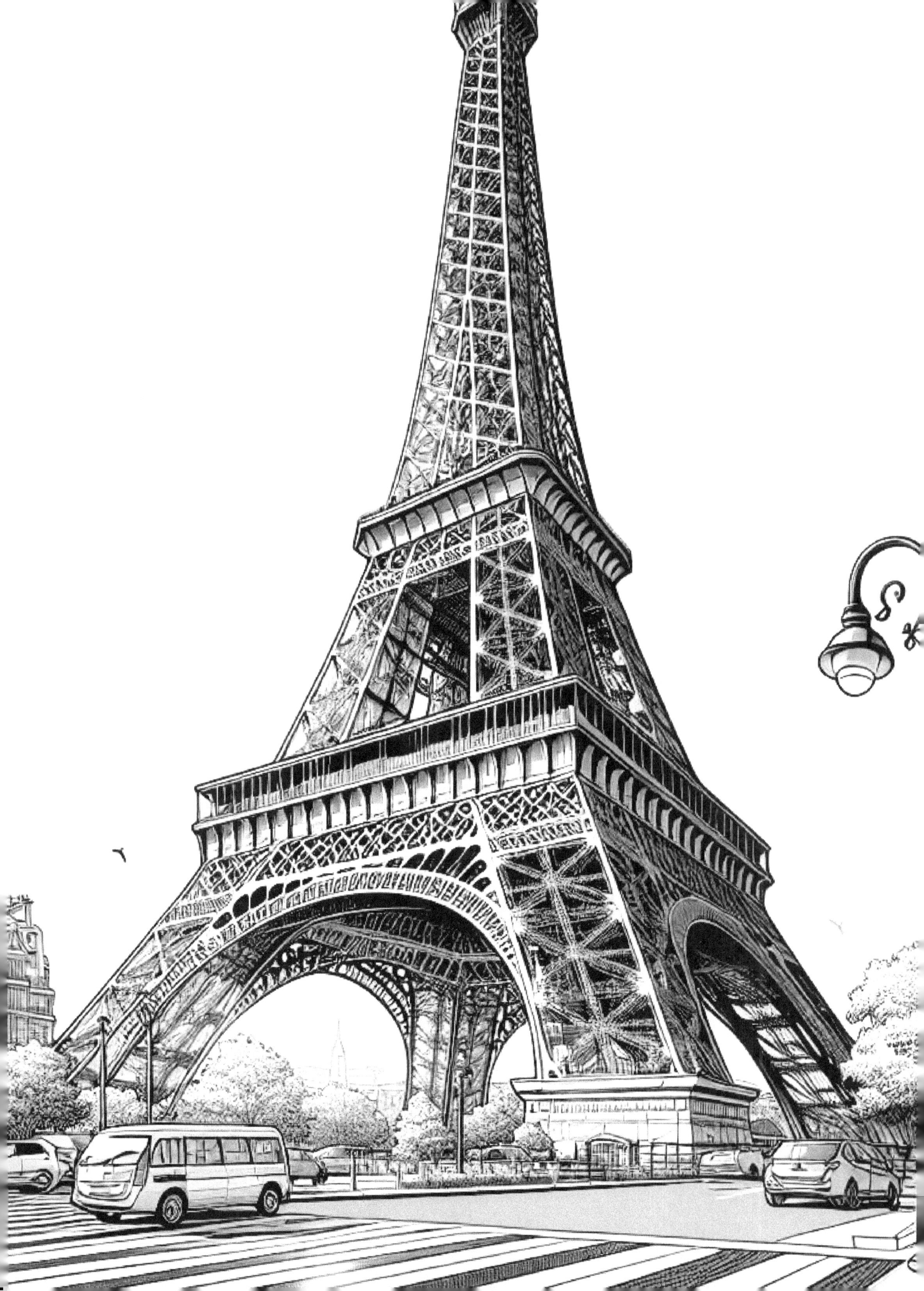

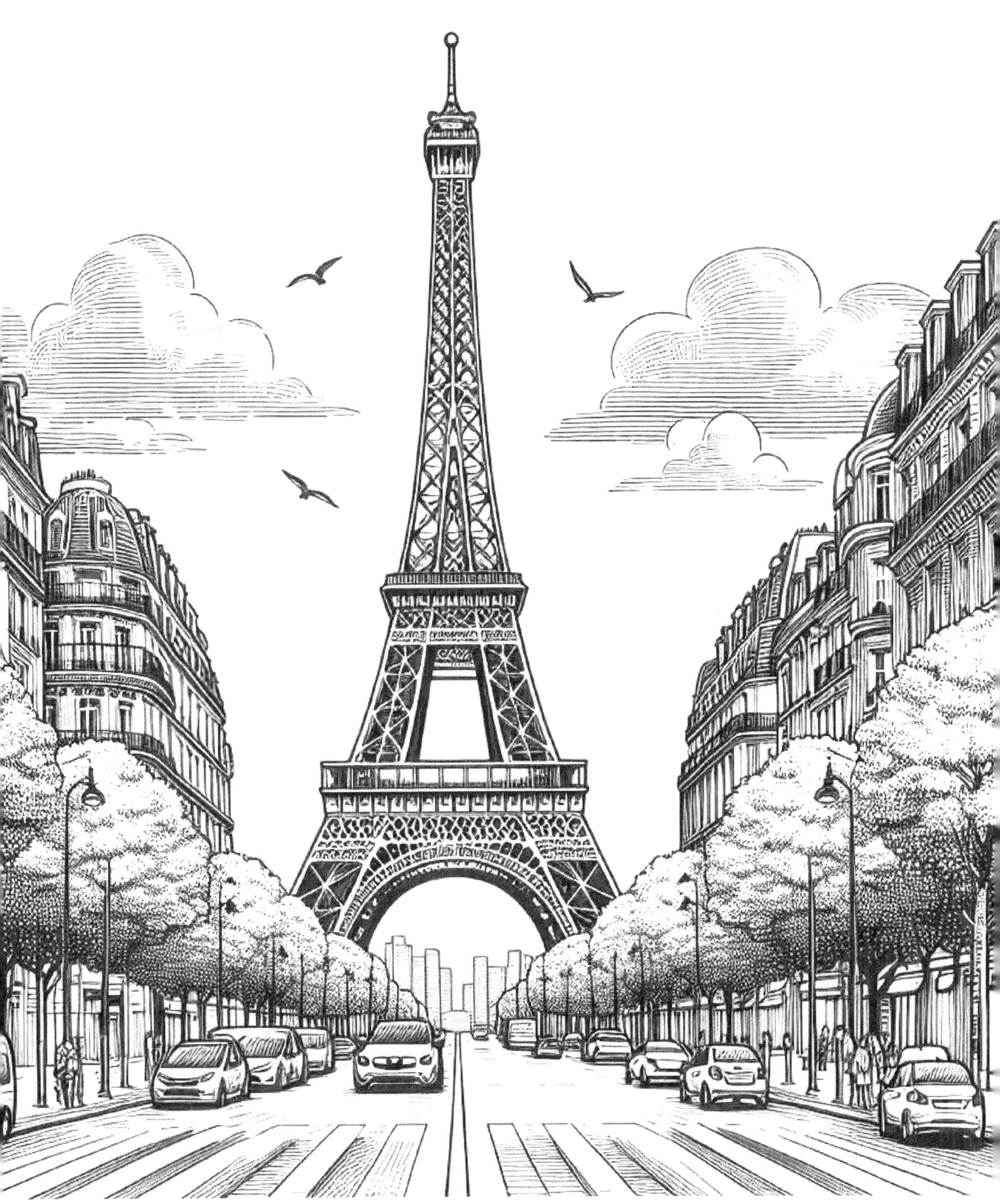

Eiffel Tower

PARIS, FRANCE

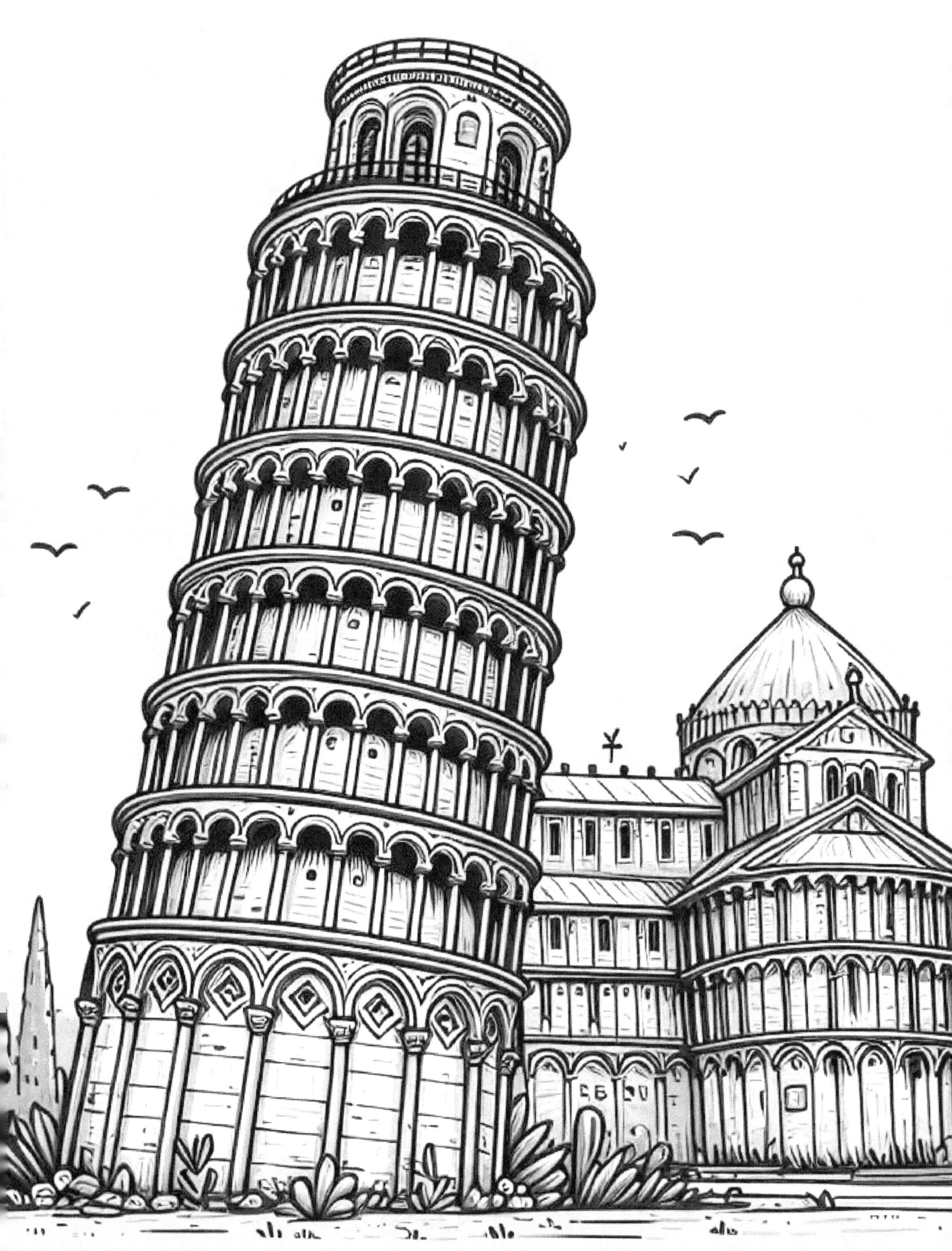

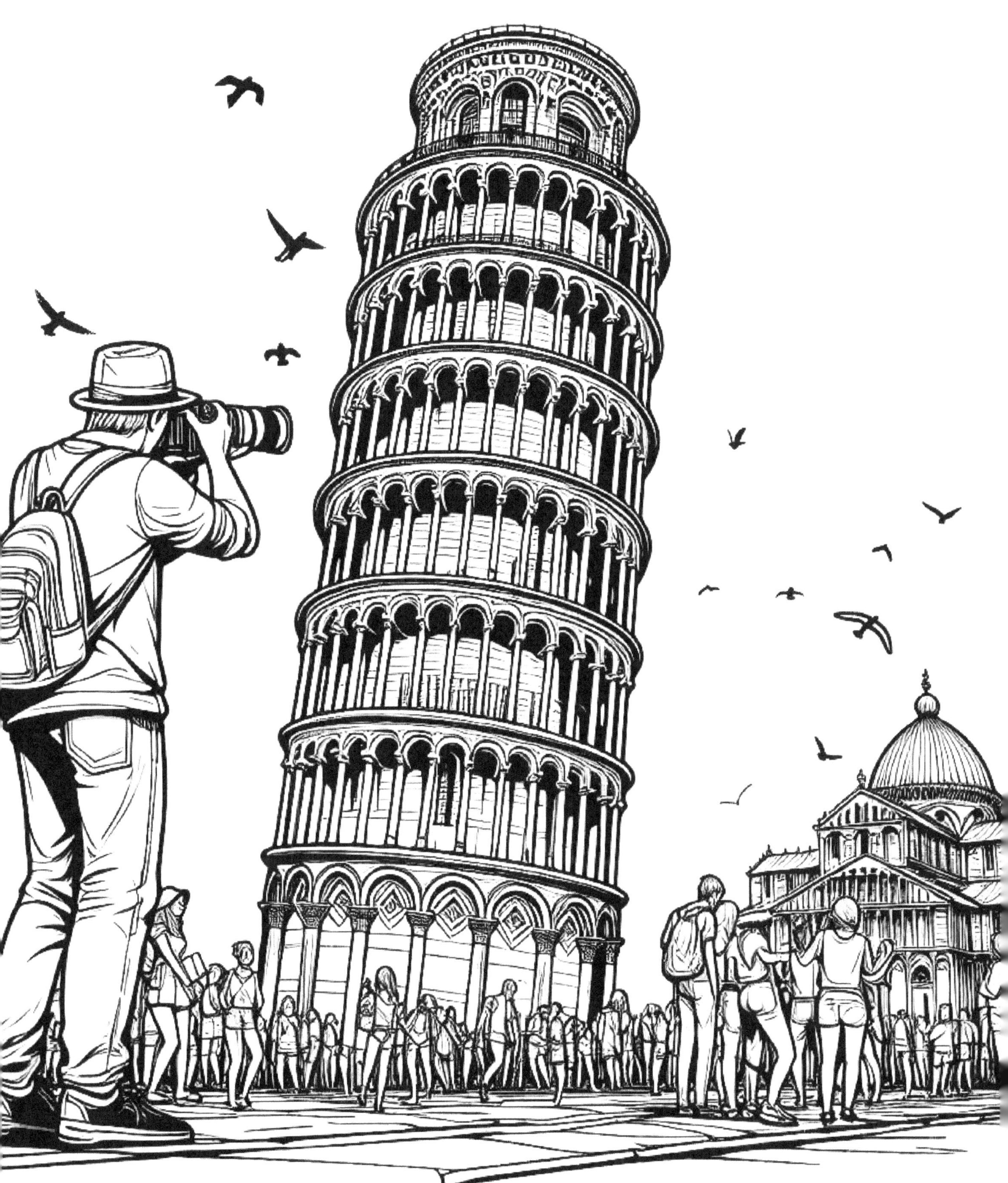

Pisa Tower

PISA, ITALY

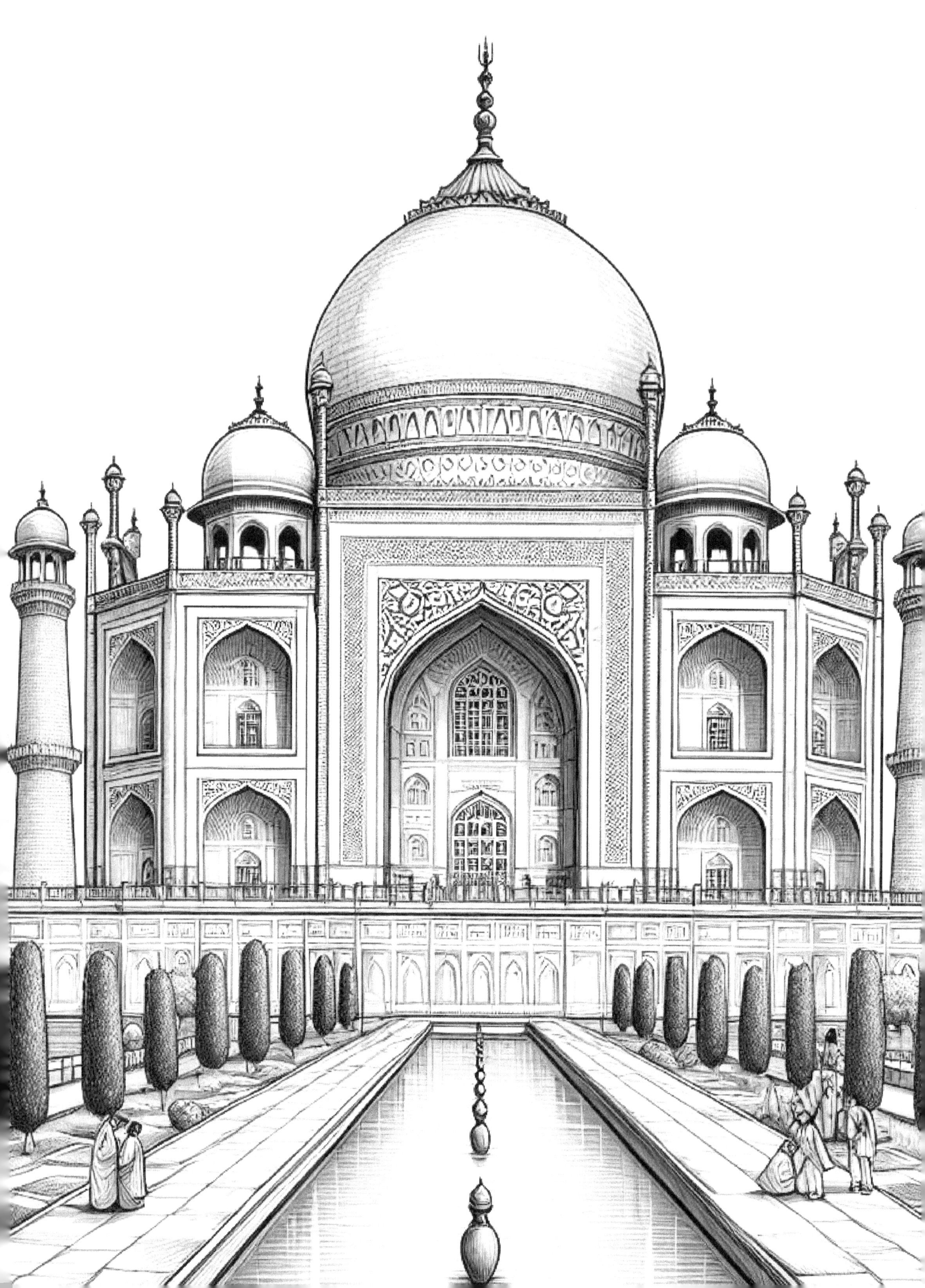

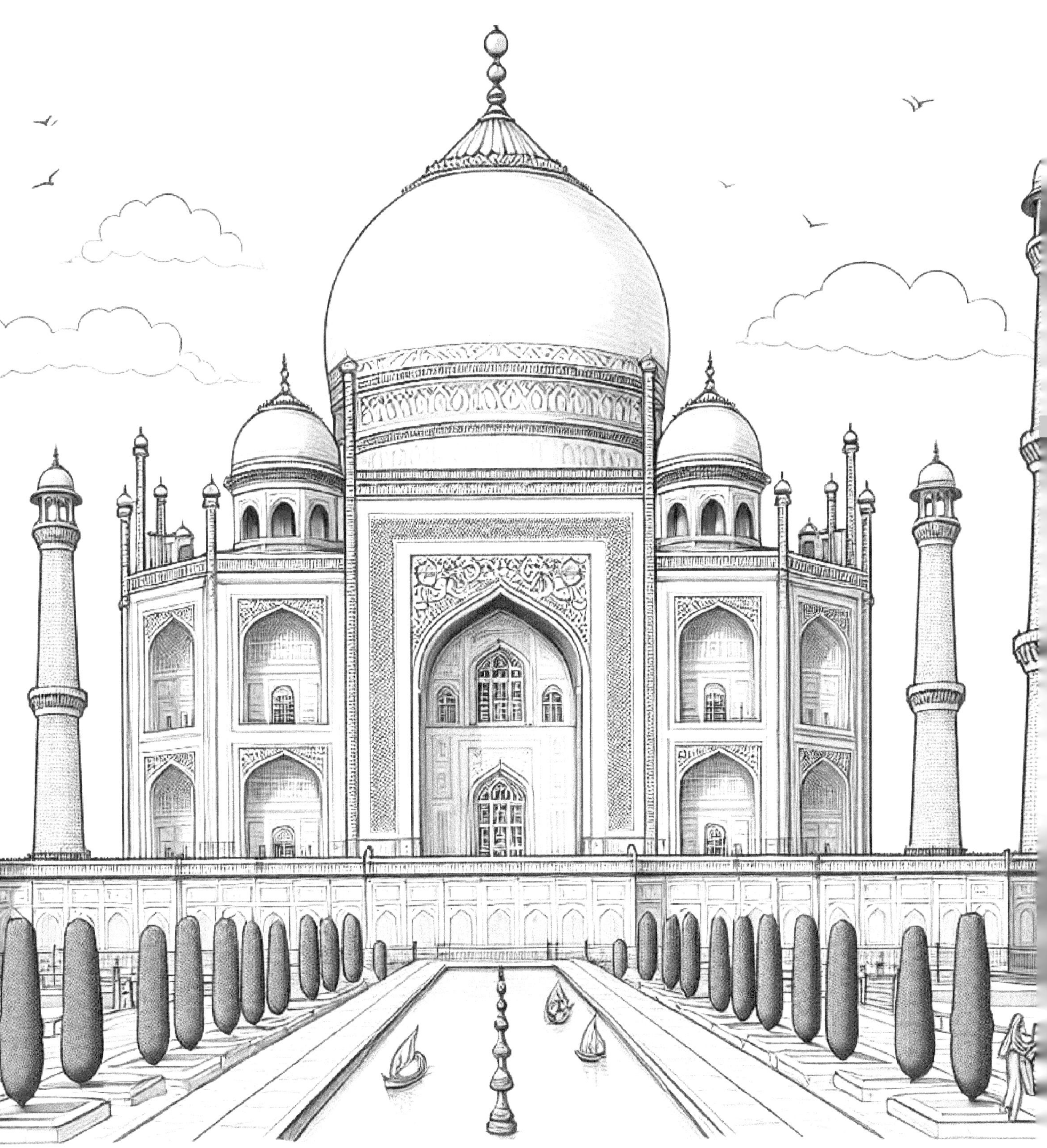

Taj Mahal

AGRA, INDIA

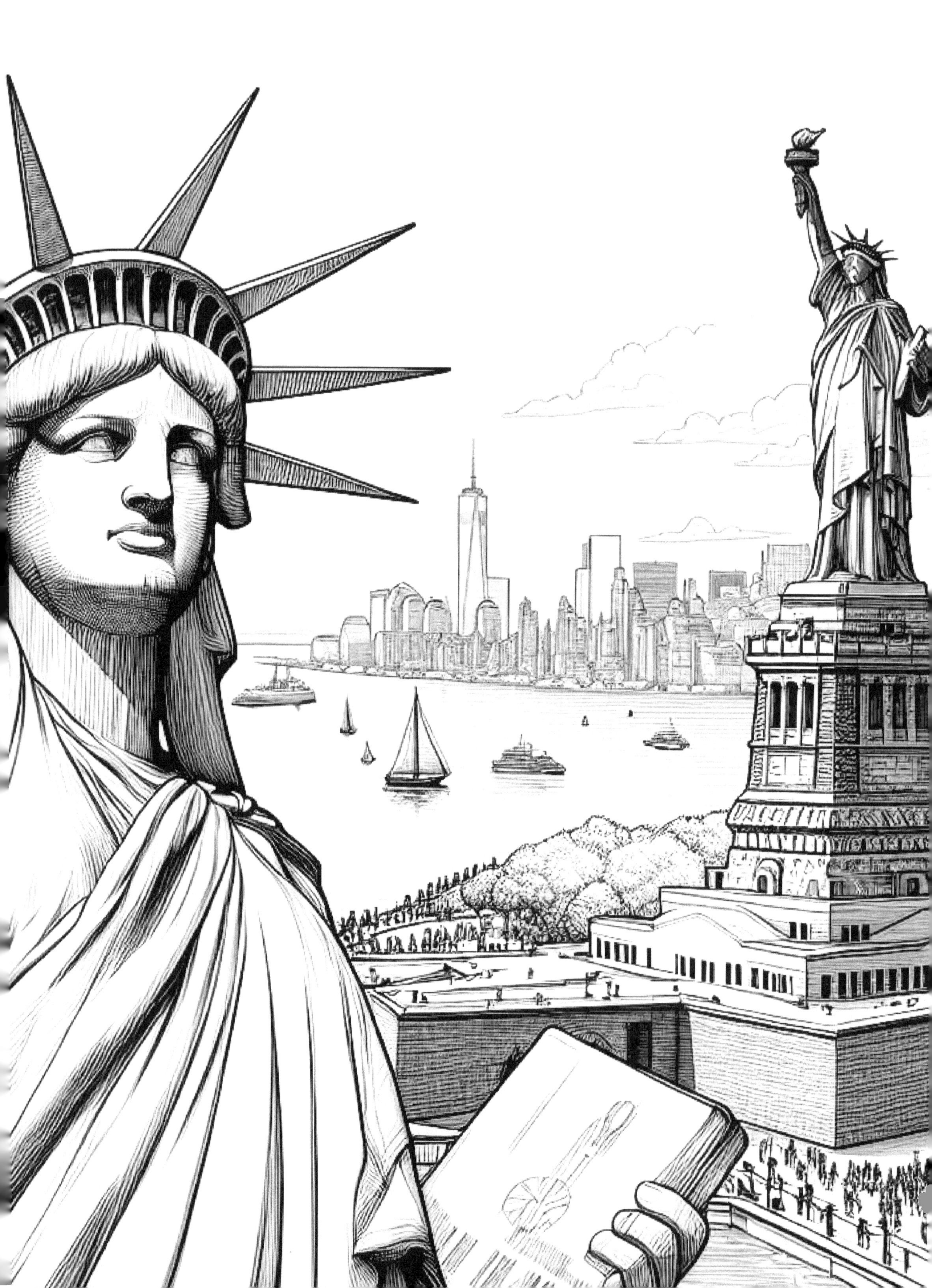

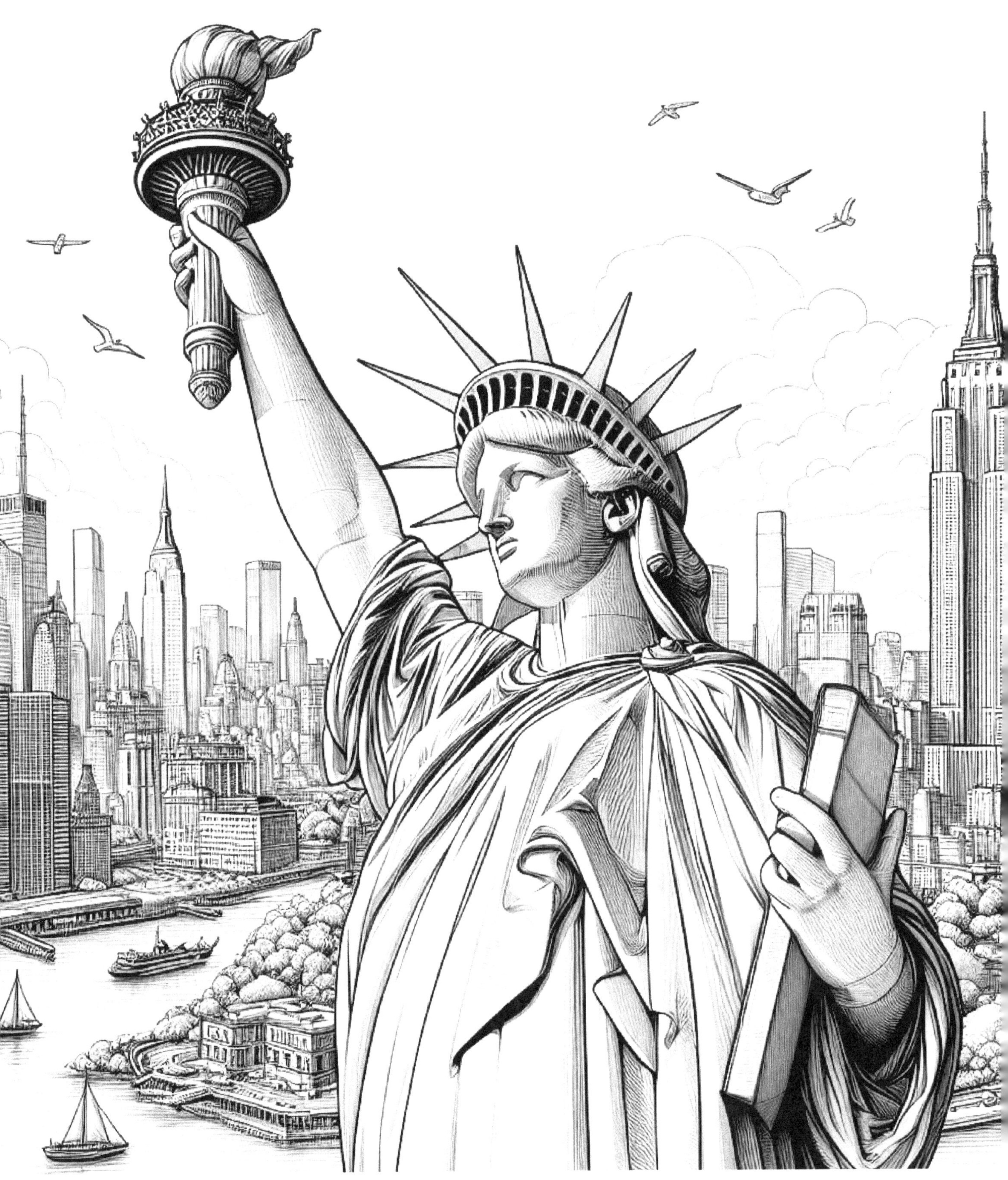

Statue of Liberty

NEW YORK, USA

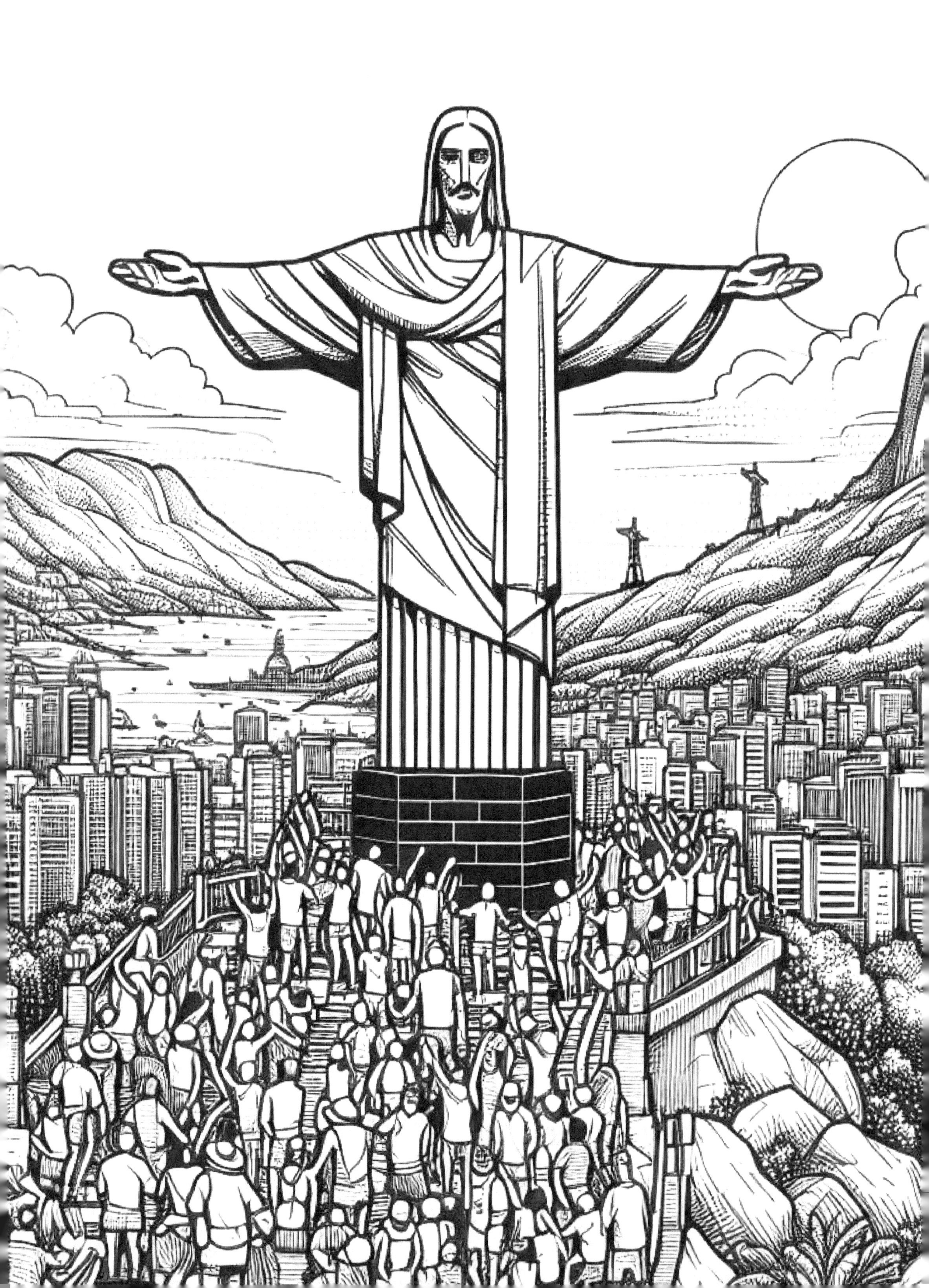

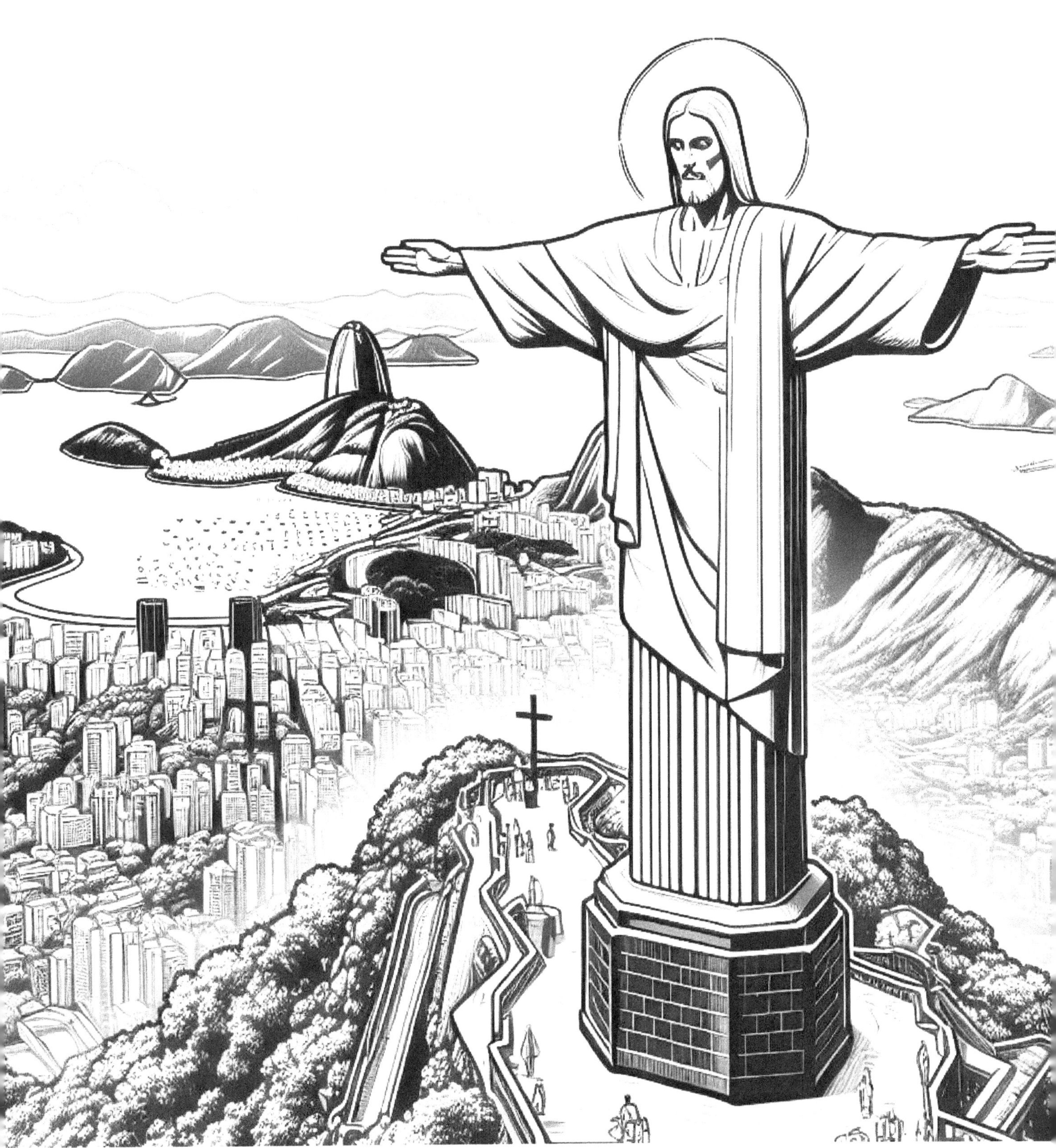

Statue of Christ
the Redeemer
RIO DE JANEIRO, BRAZIL

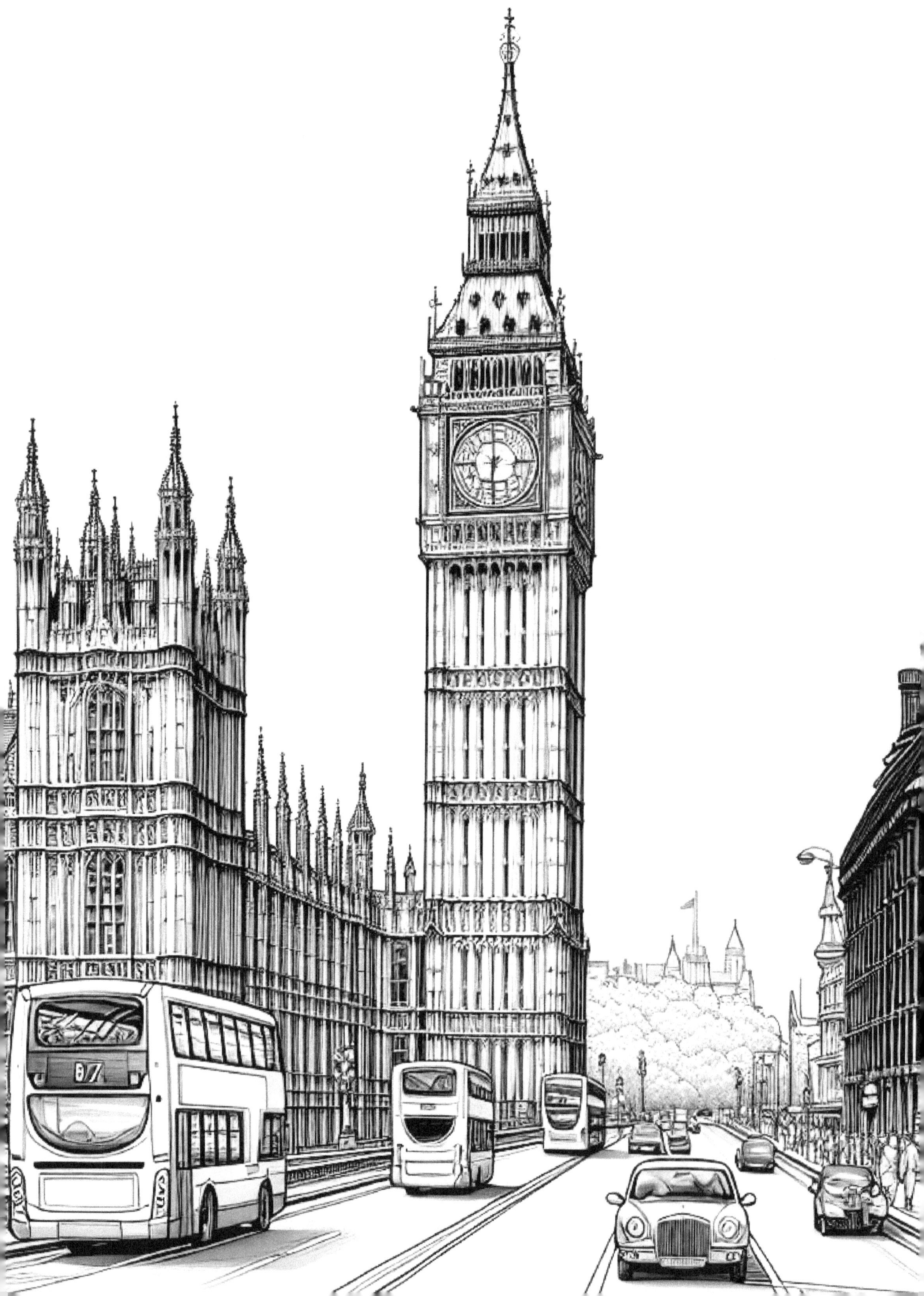

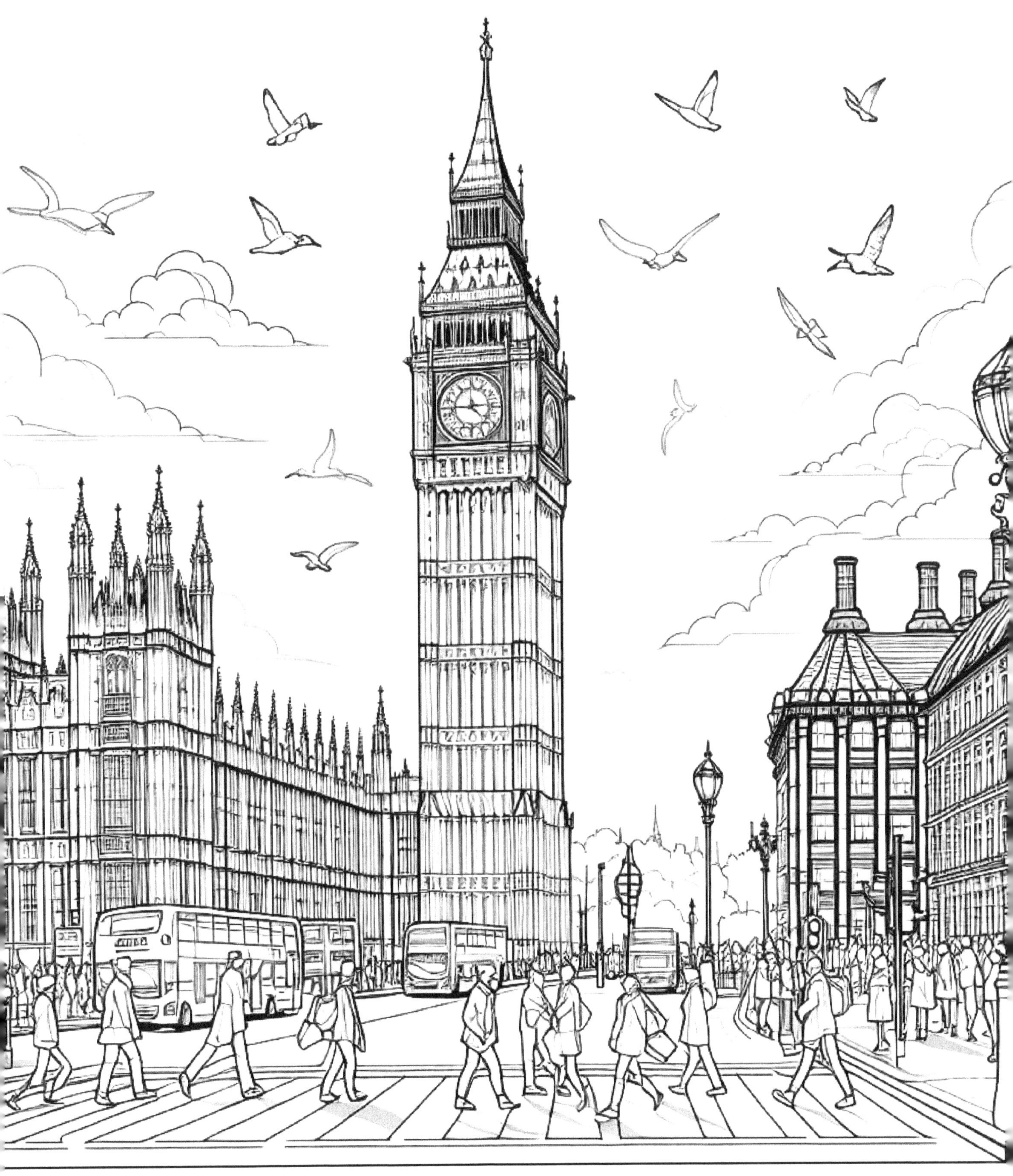

Big Ben
LONDON, UK

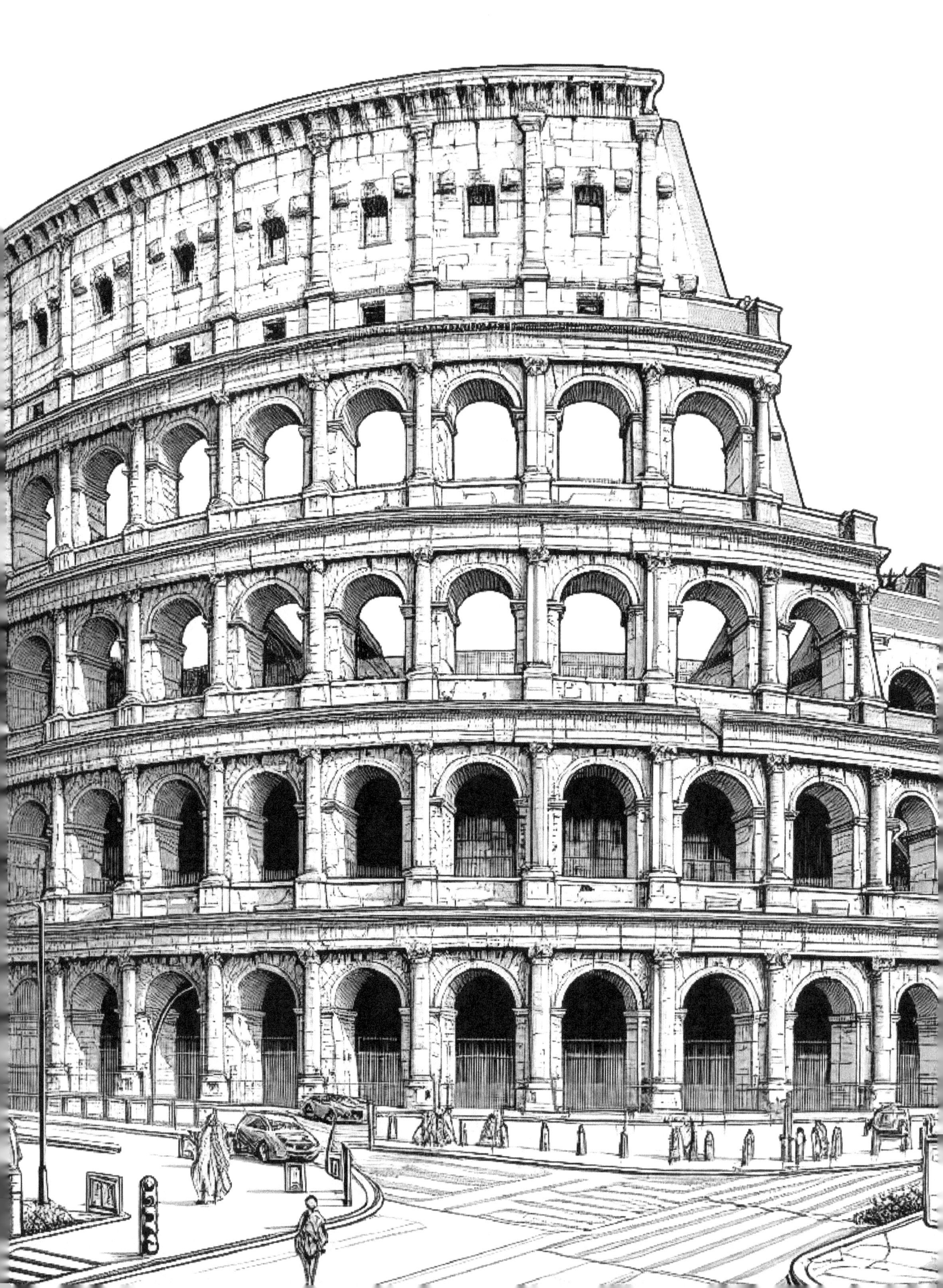

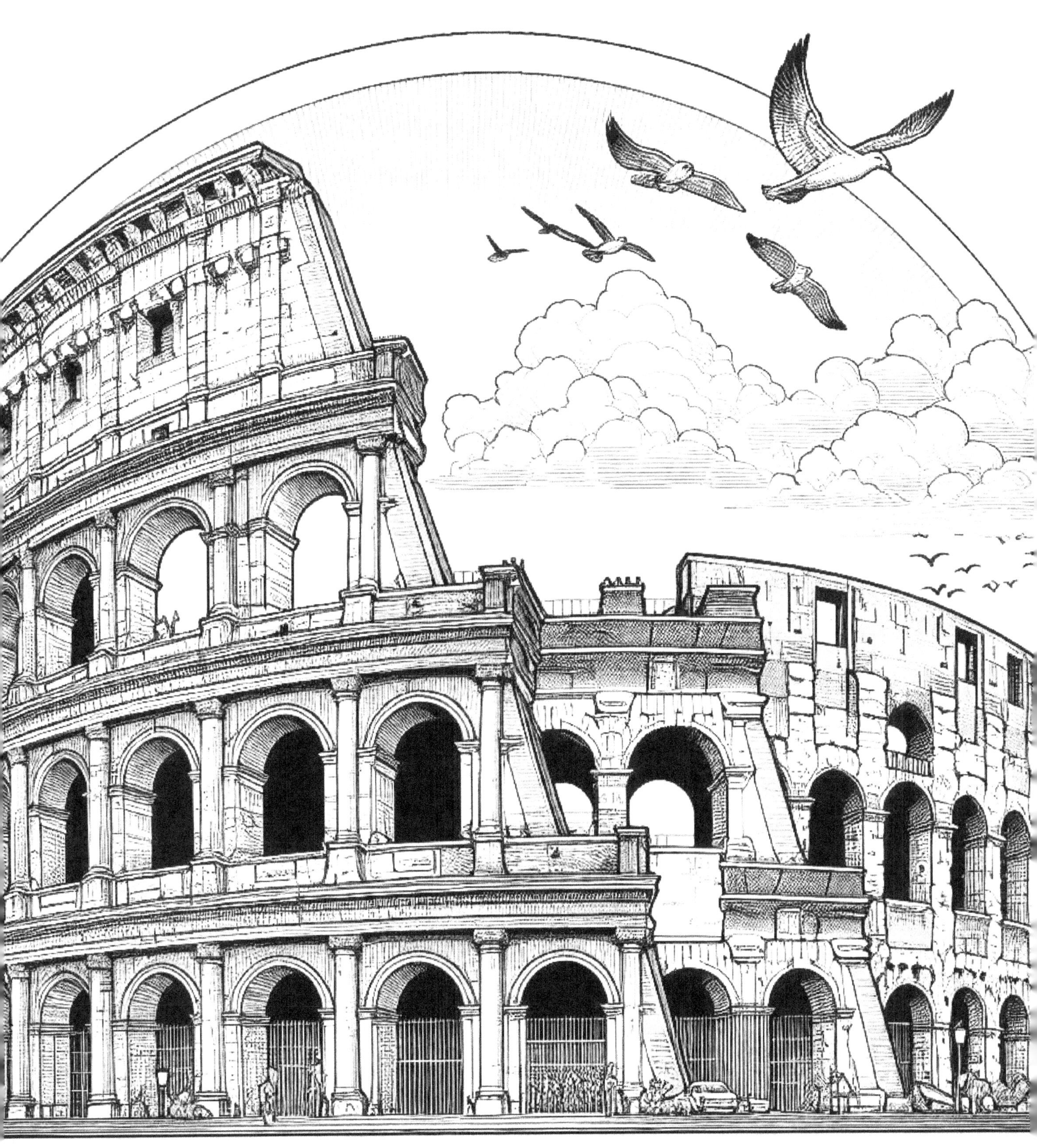

Coliseum
ROME, ITALY

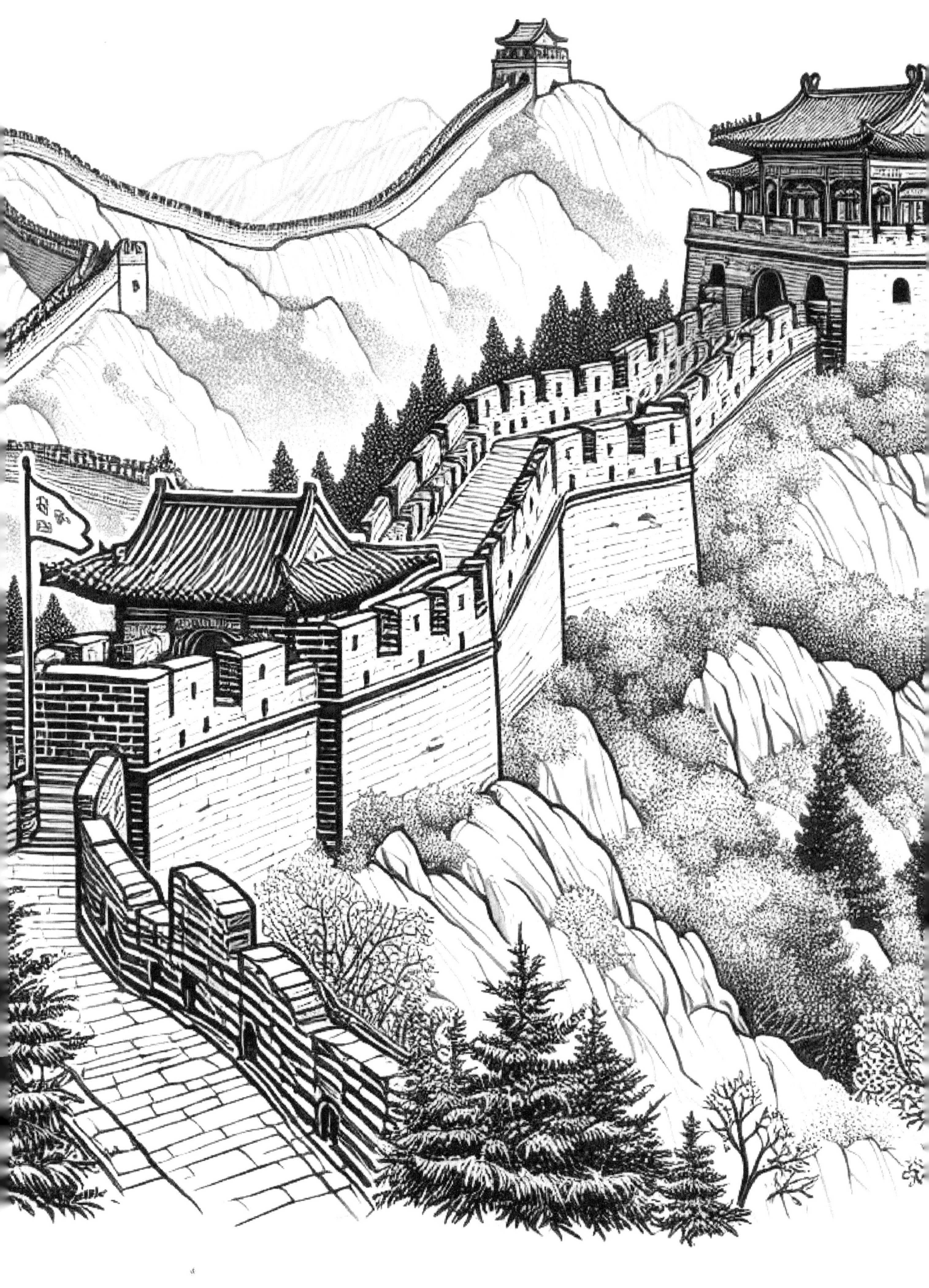

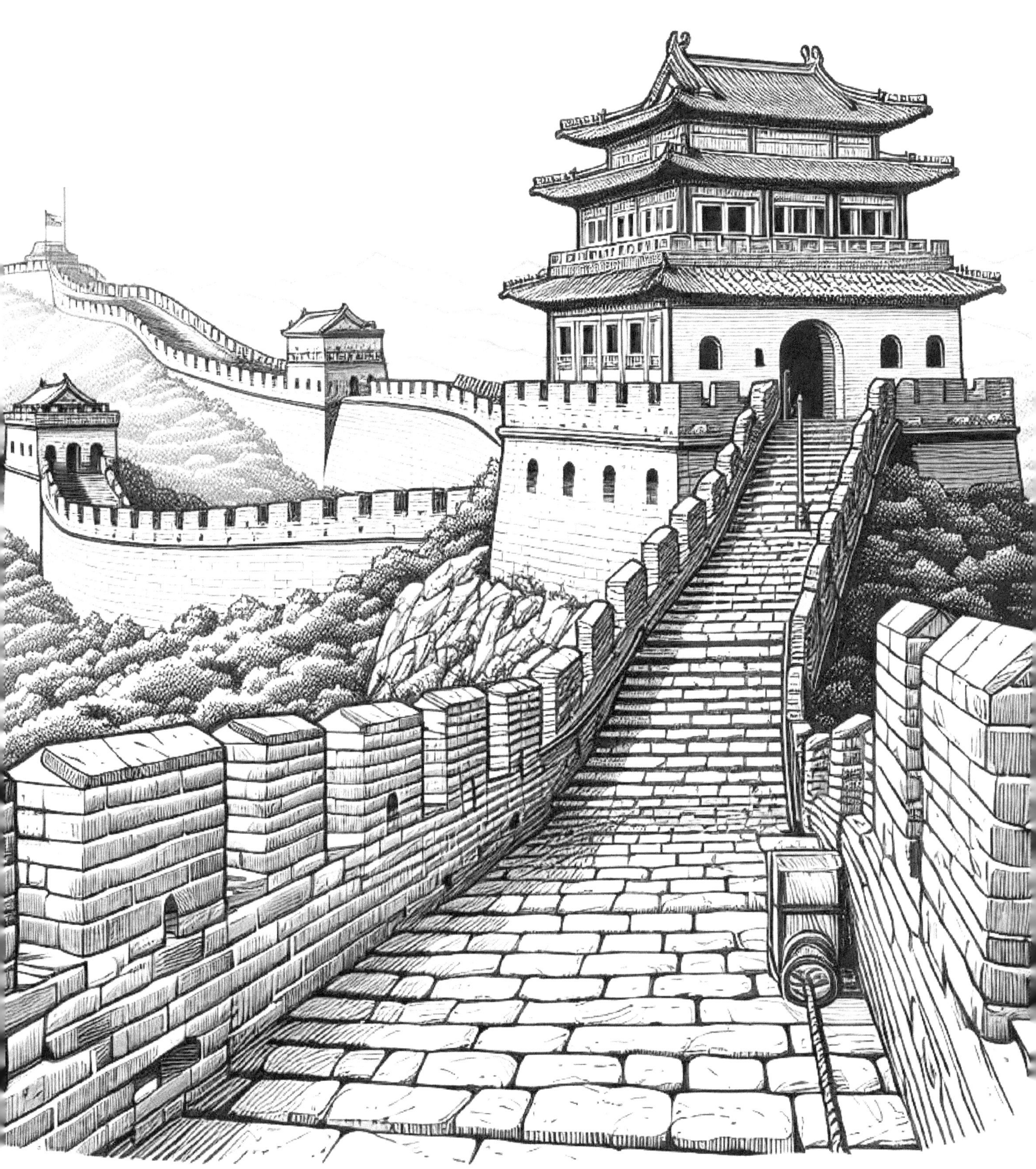

Great Wall of China

BEIJING, CHINA

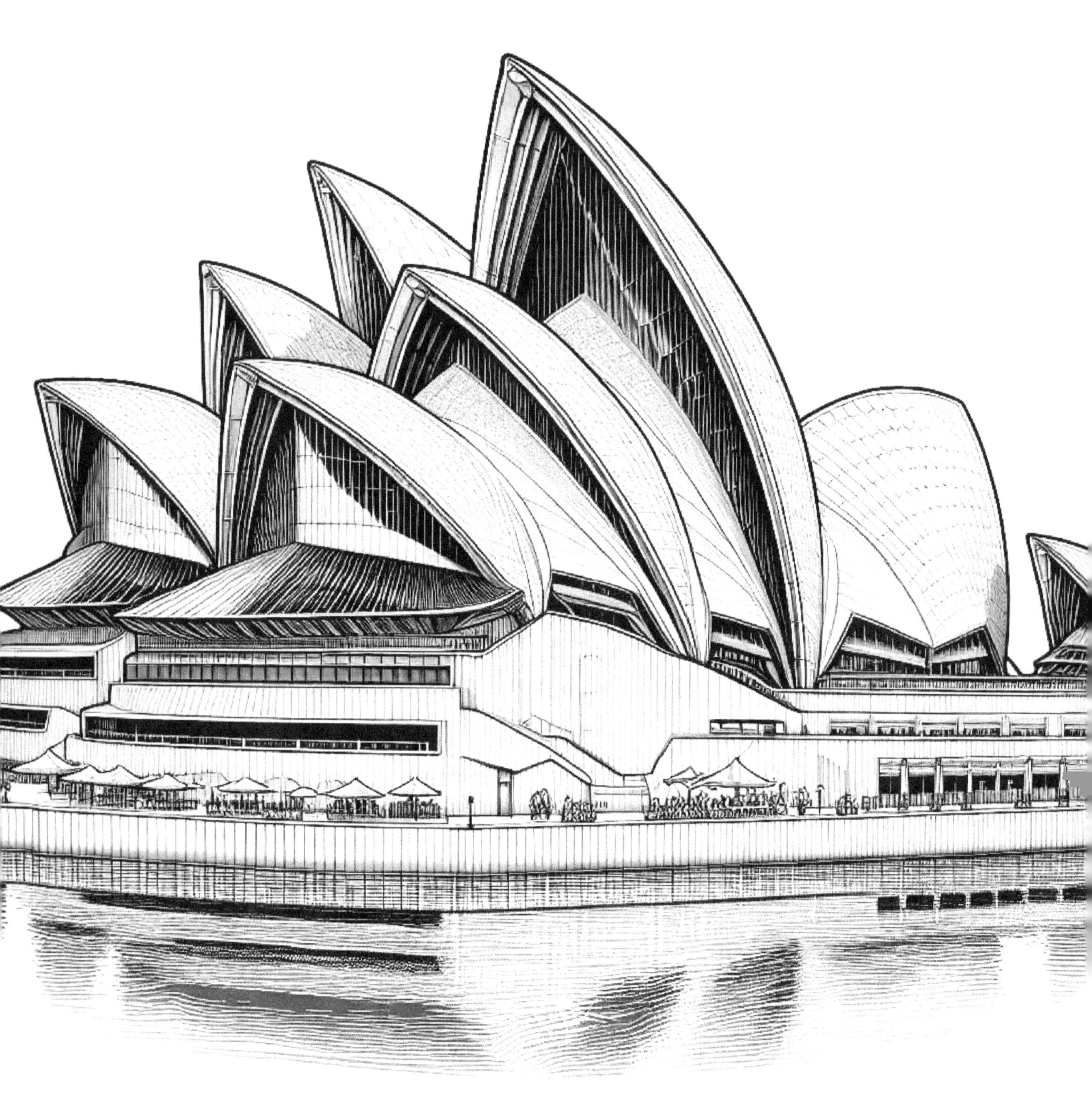

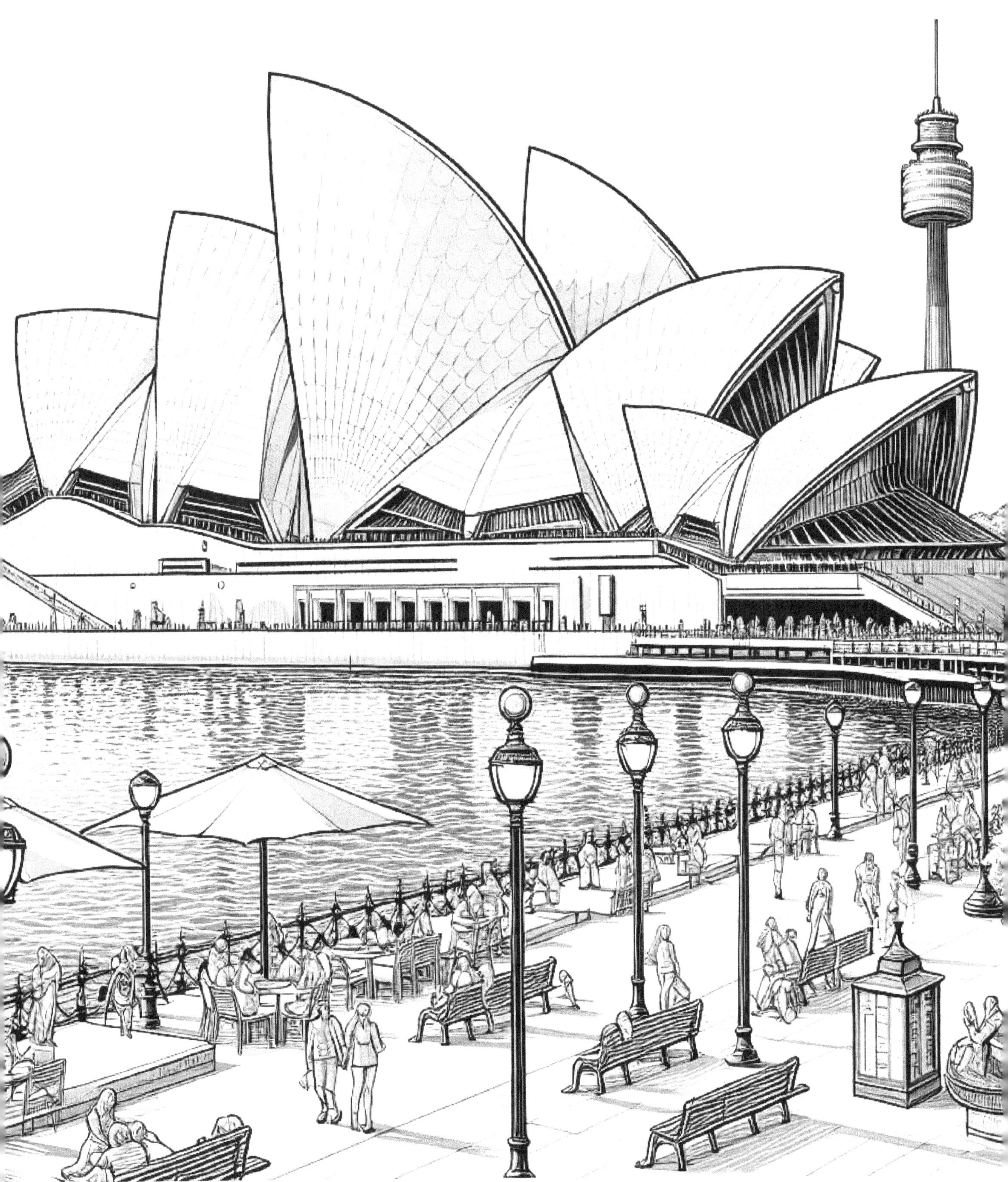

Sidney Opera House

SIDNEY, AUSTRALIE

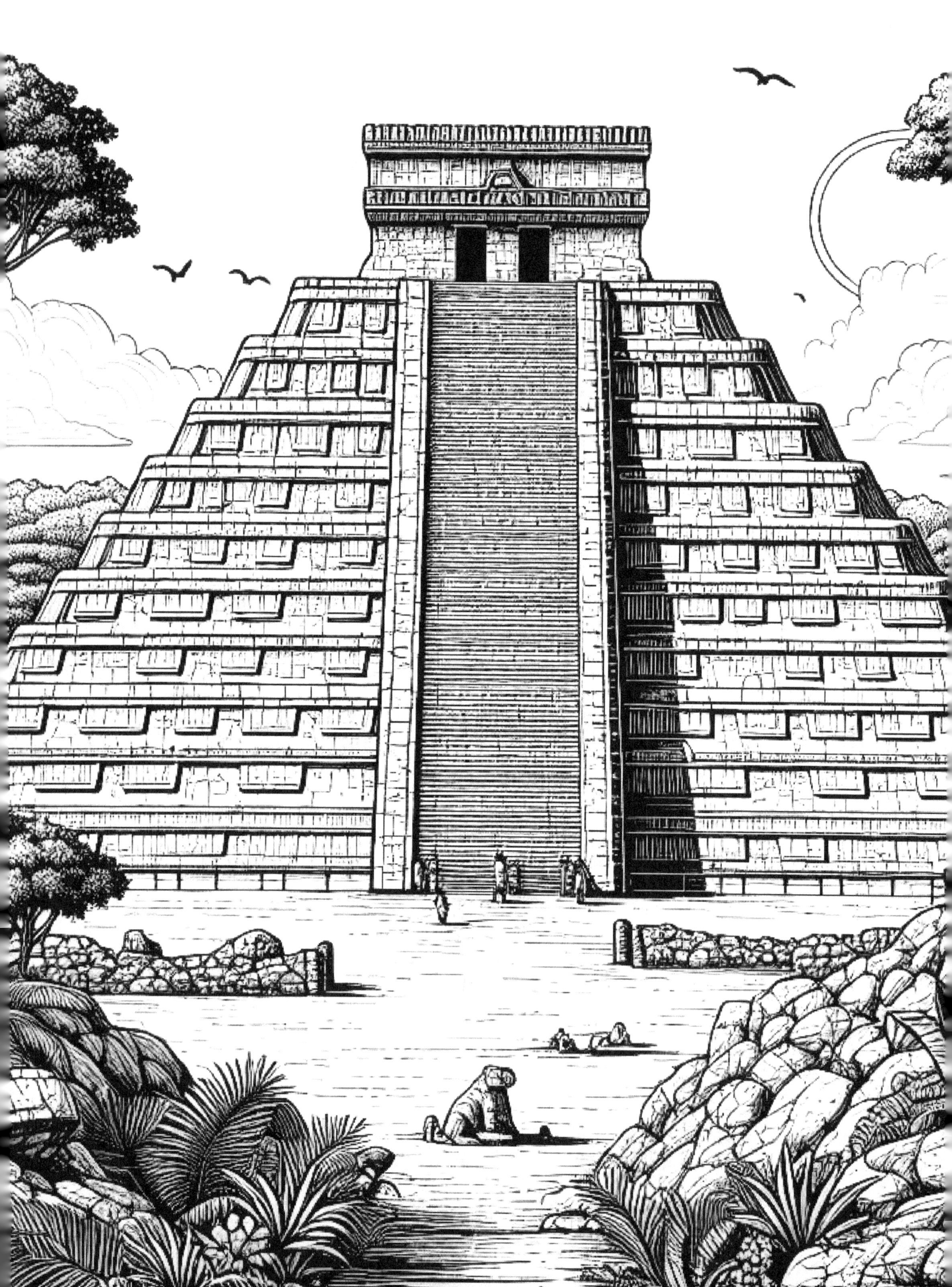

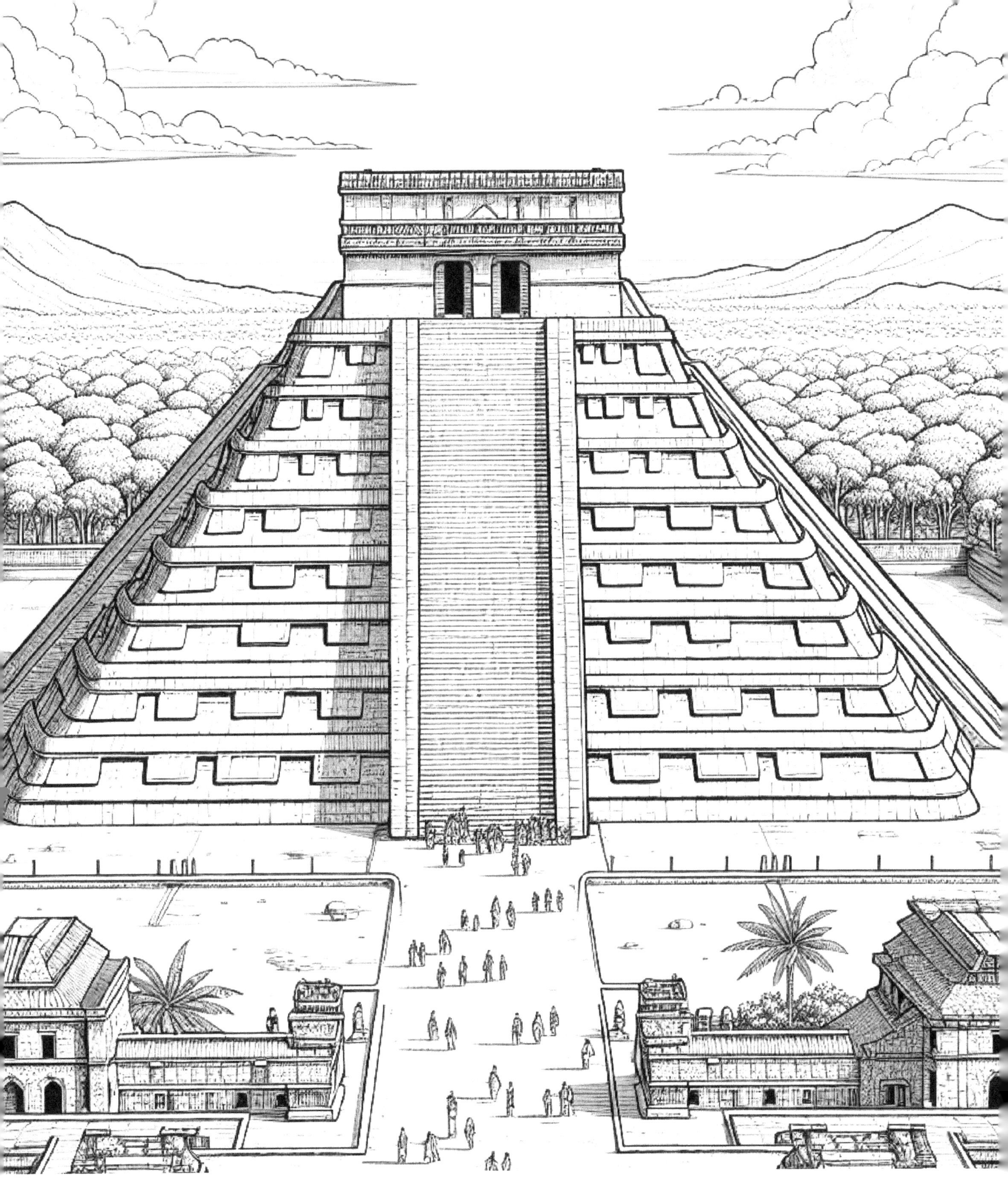

Chichén Itzá

YUCATAN, MEXICO

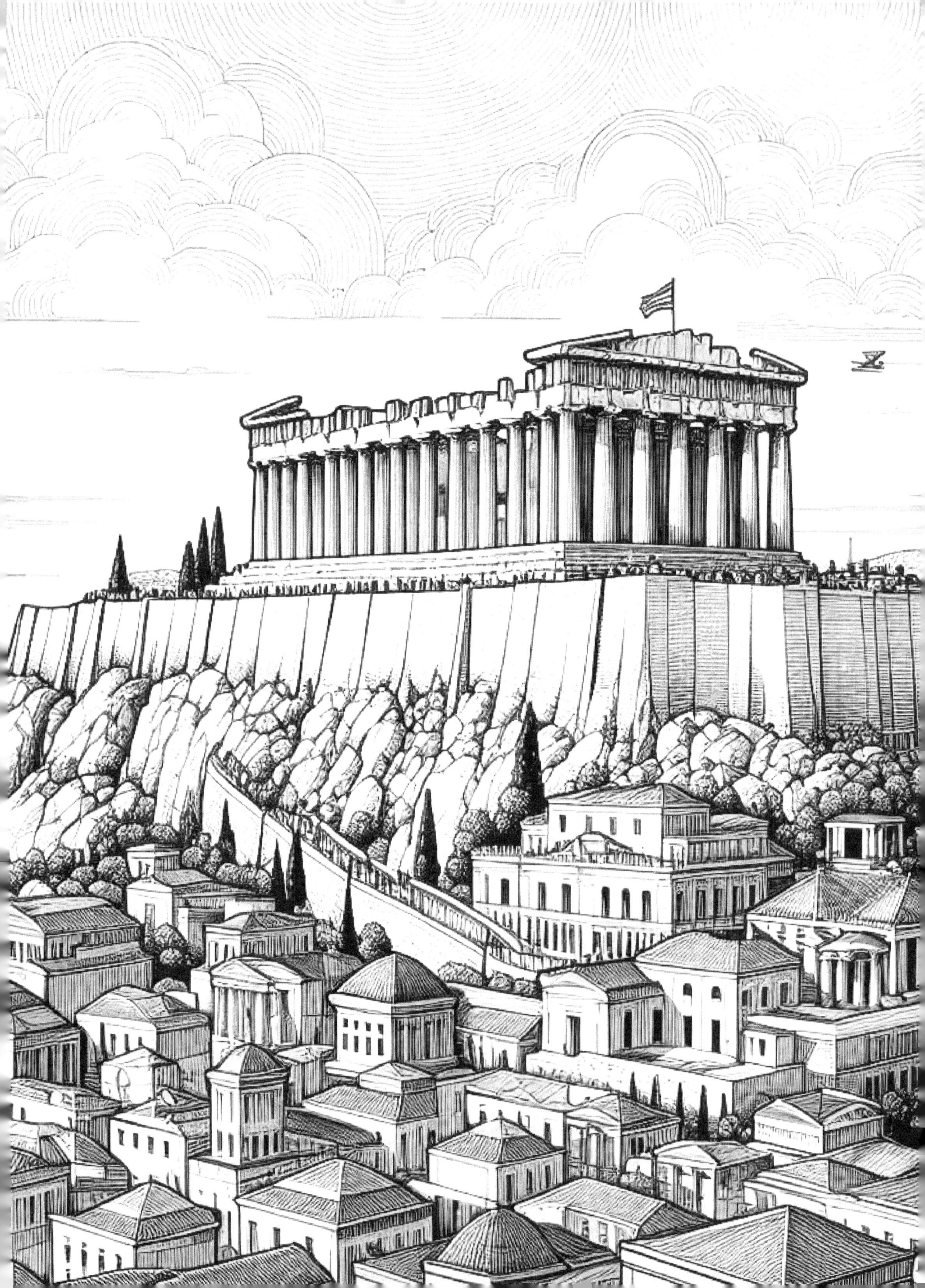

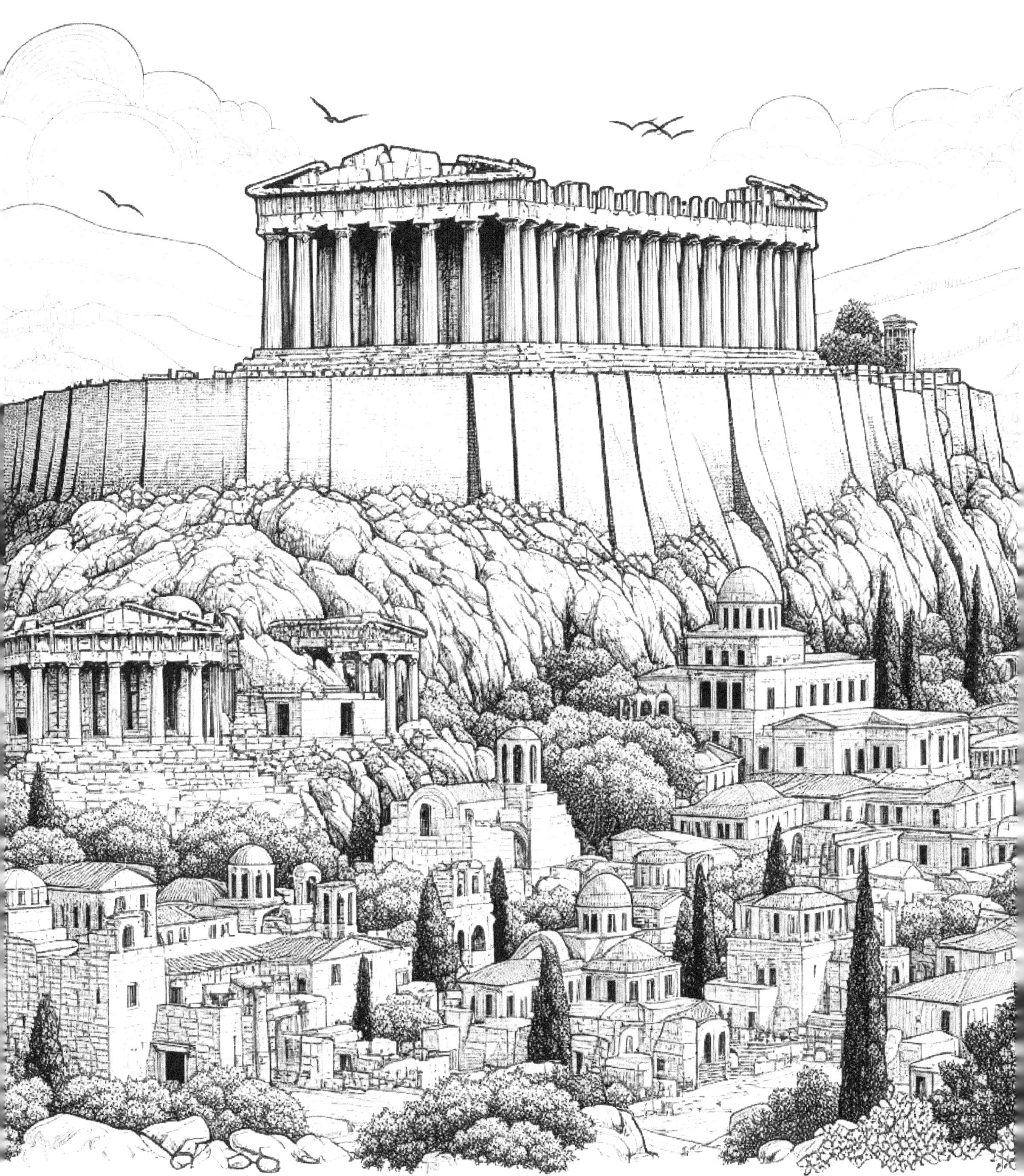

Parthenon

ATHENS, GREECE

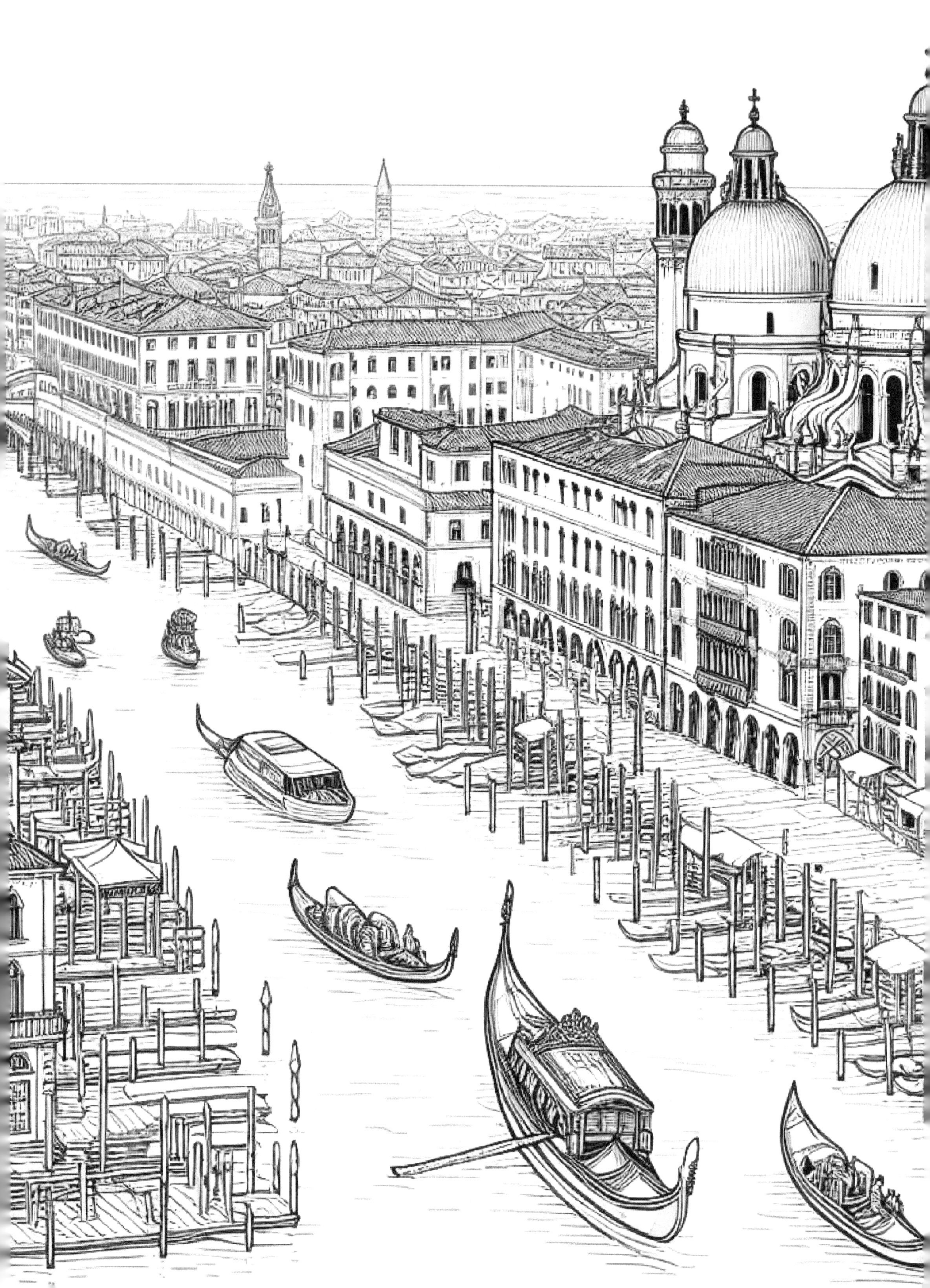

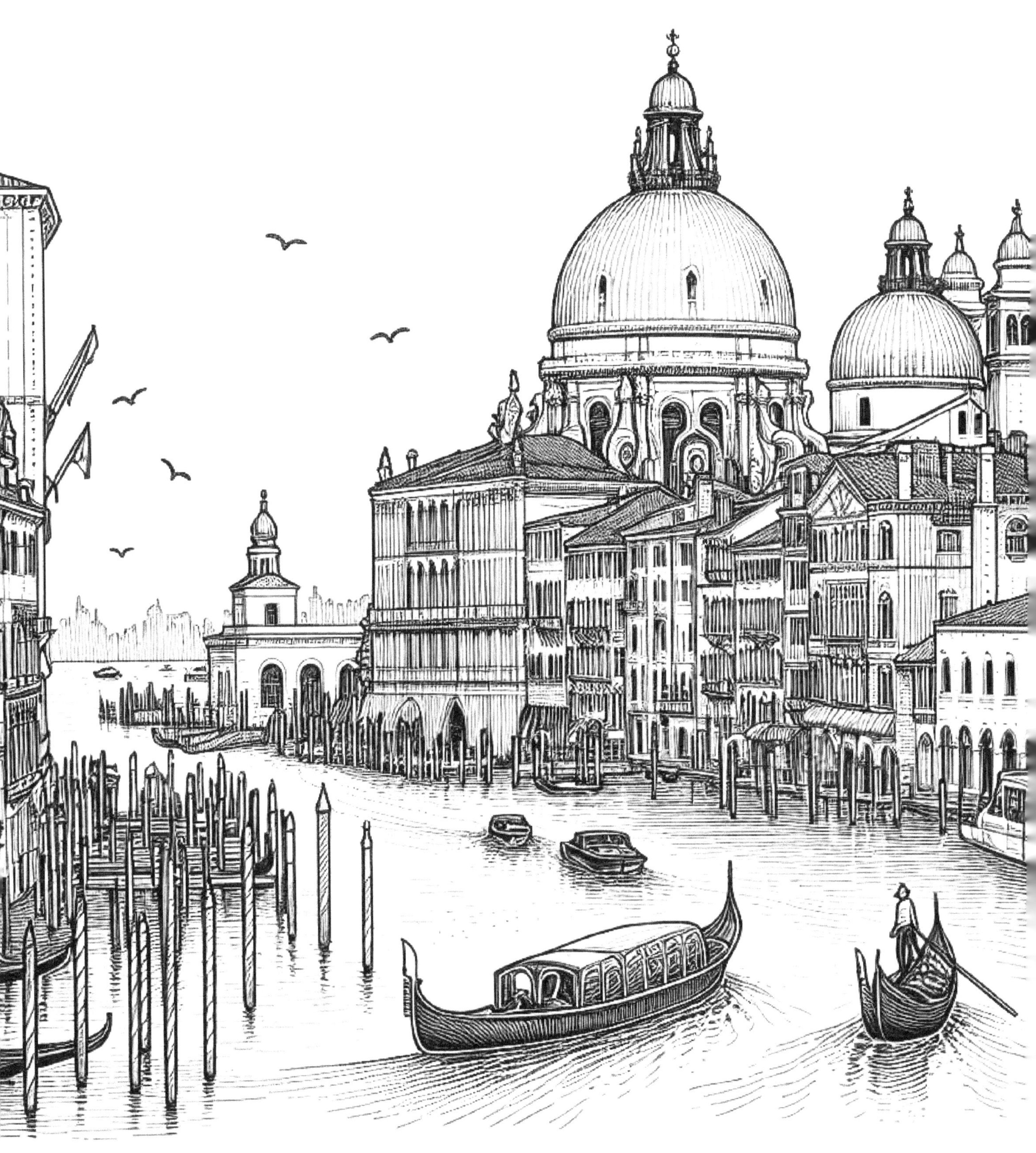

Venice

VENICE, ITALY

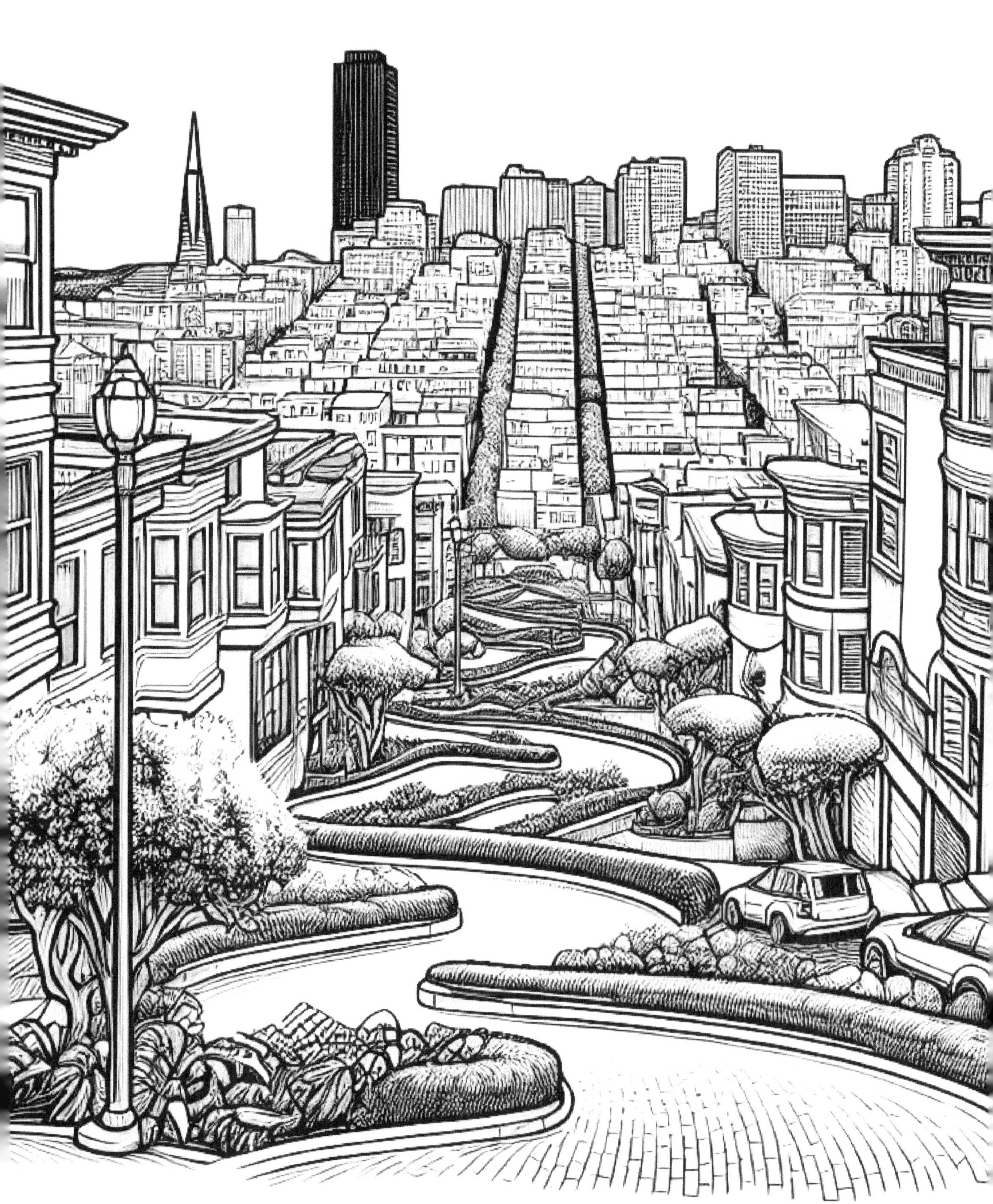

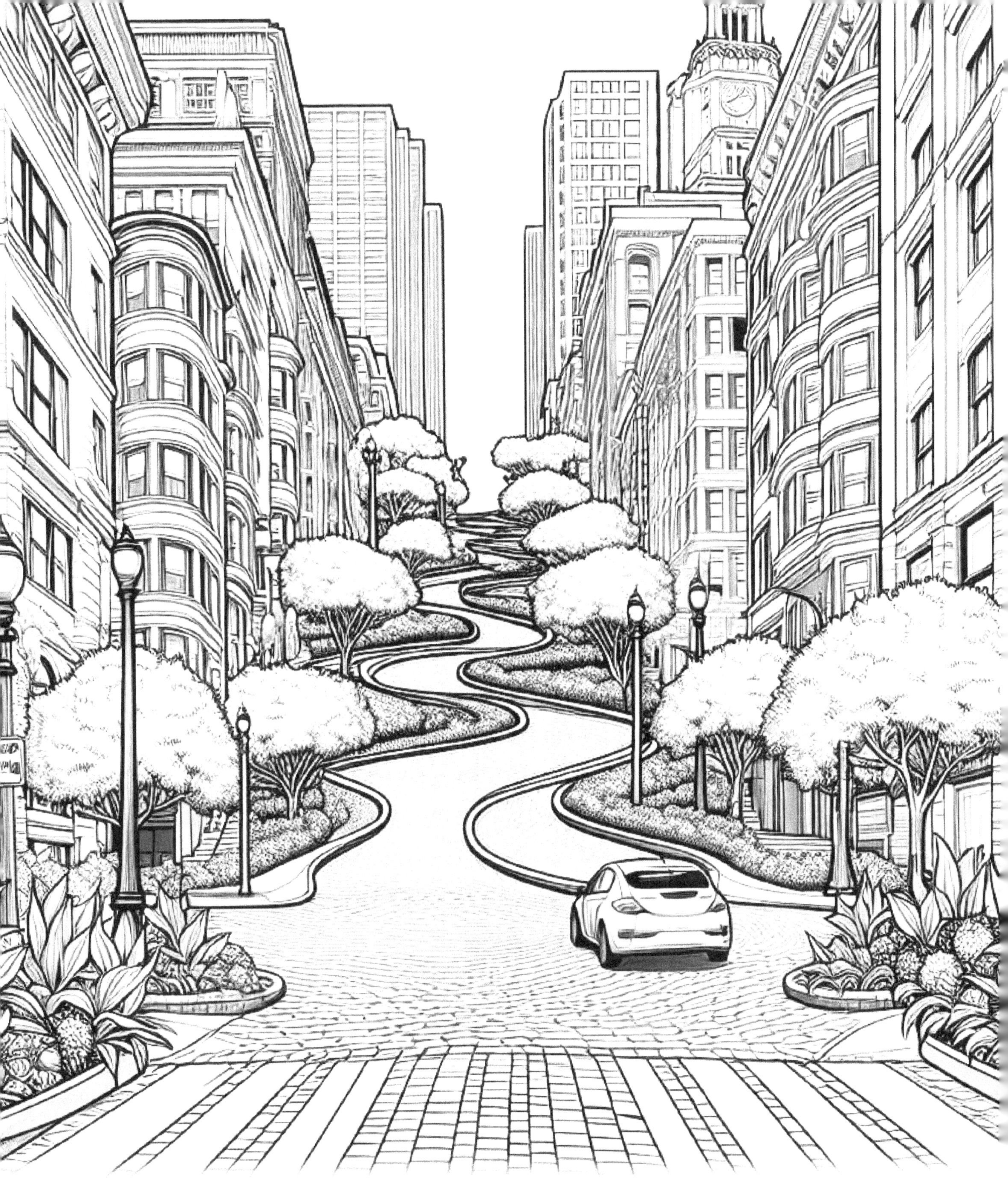

Lombard Street

SAN FRANCISCO, USA

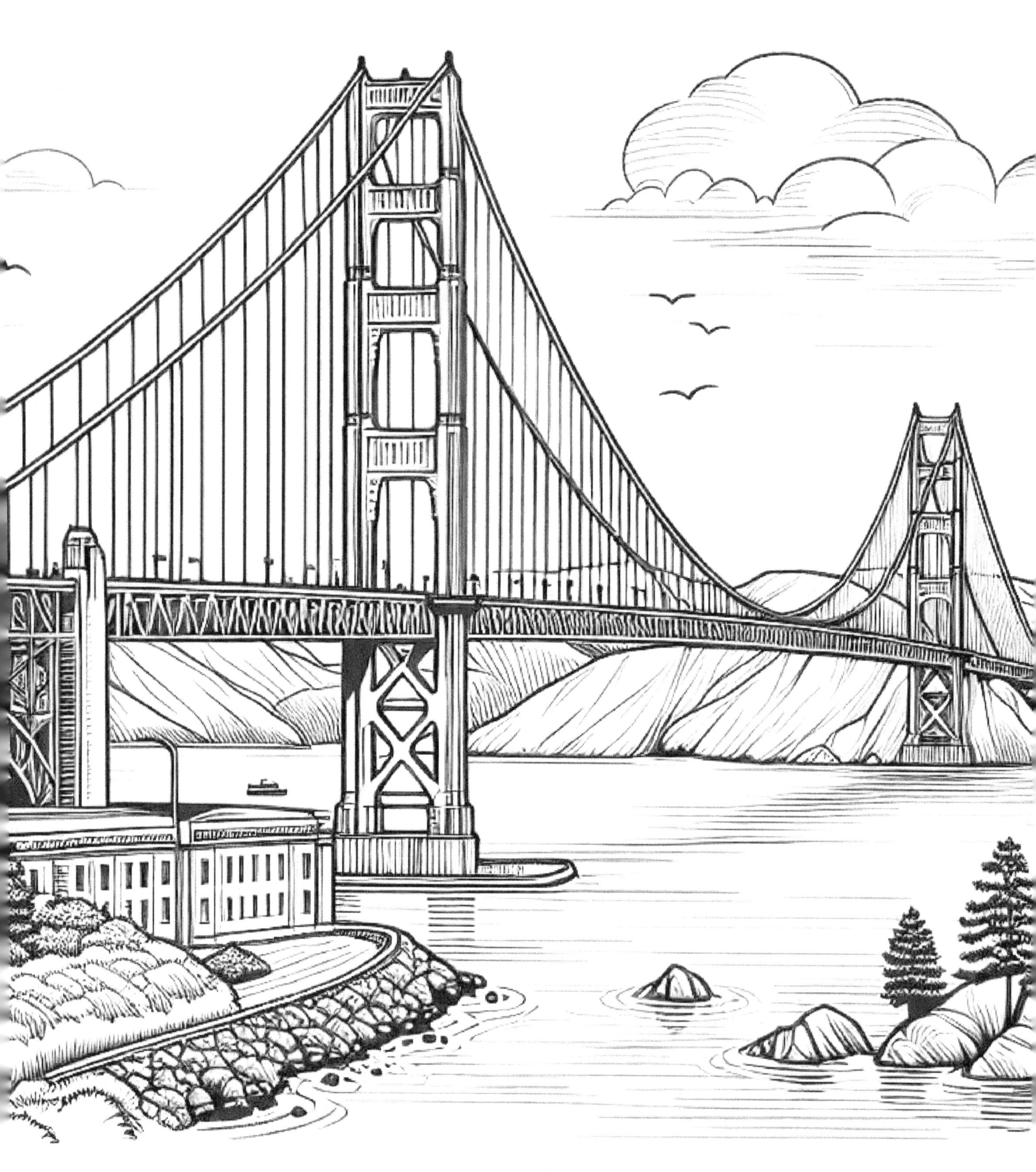

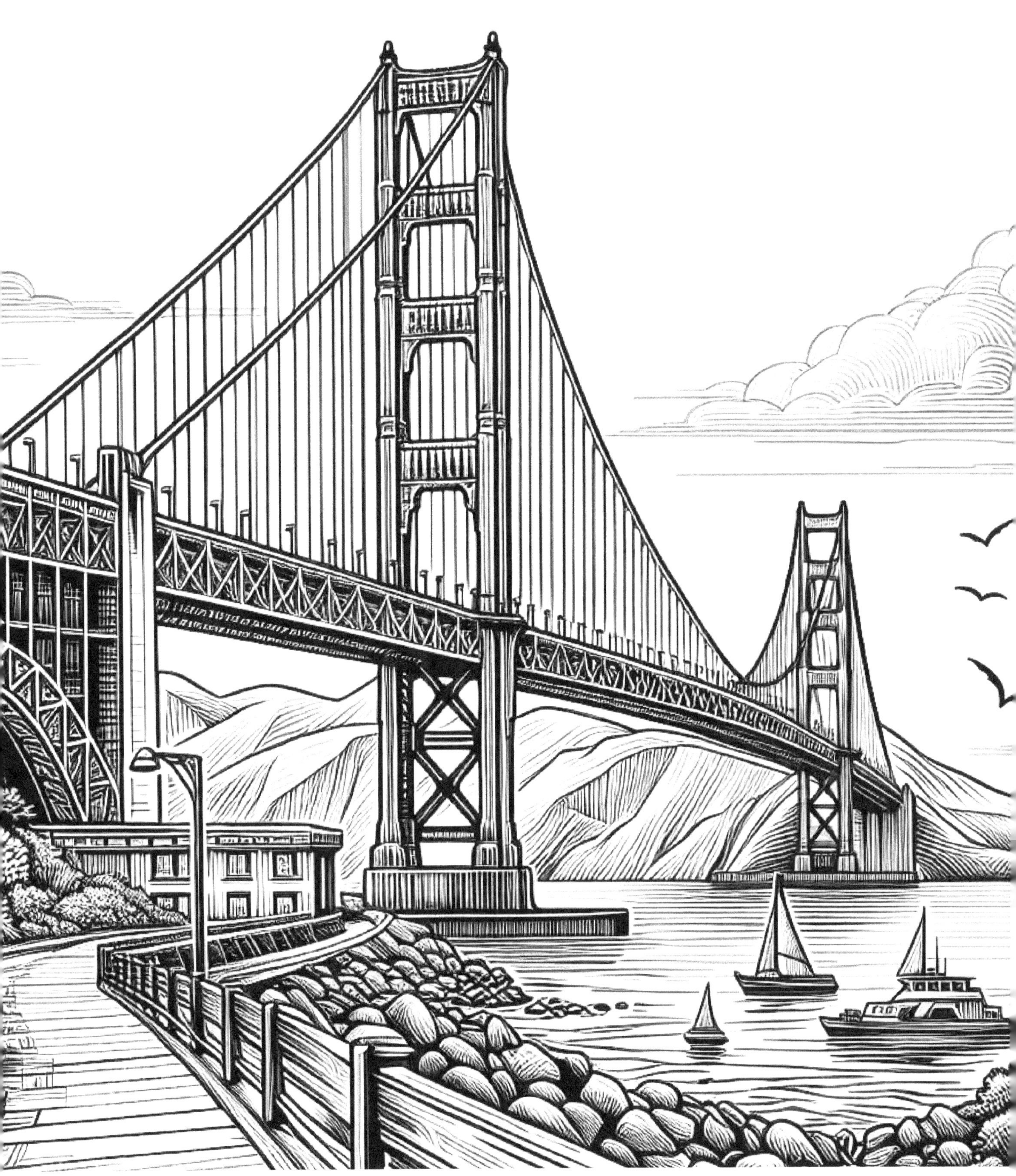

Golden Gate

CALIFORNIA, USA

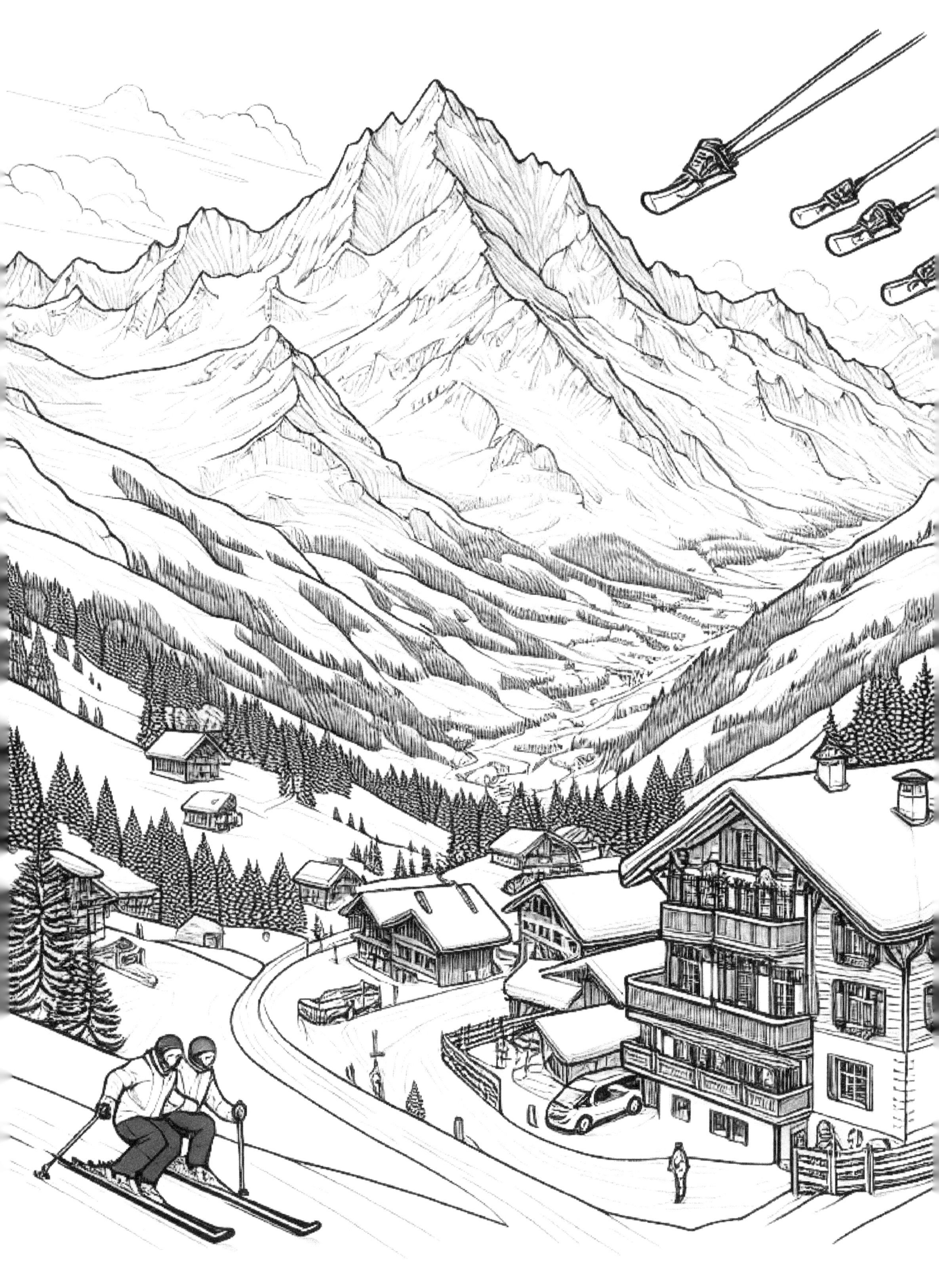

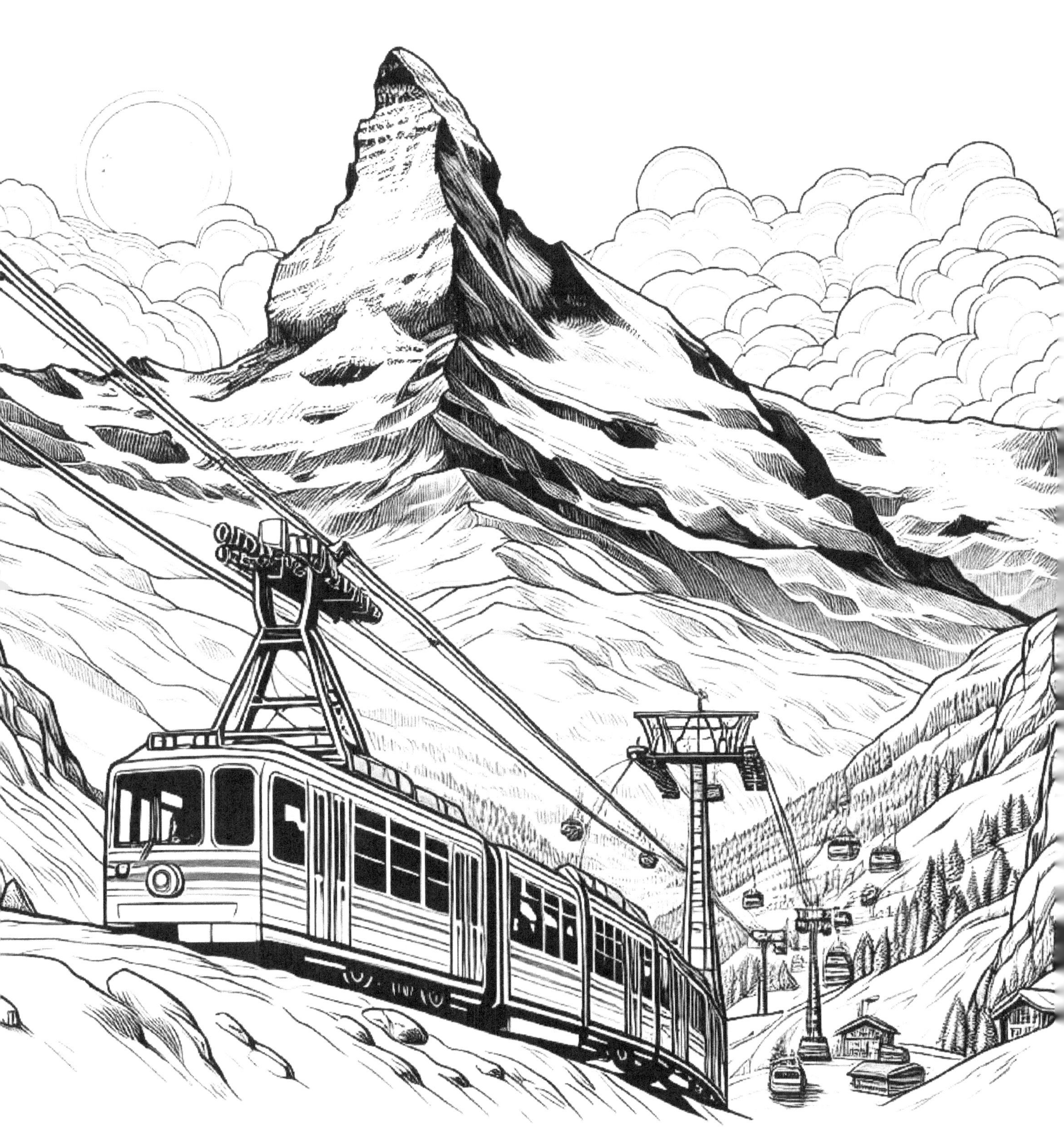

Matterhorn and Alps

ZERMATT, SWITZERLAND

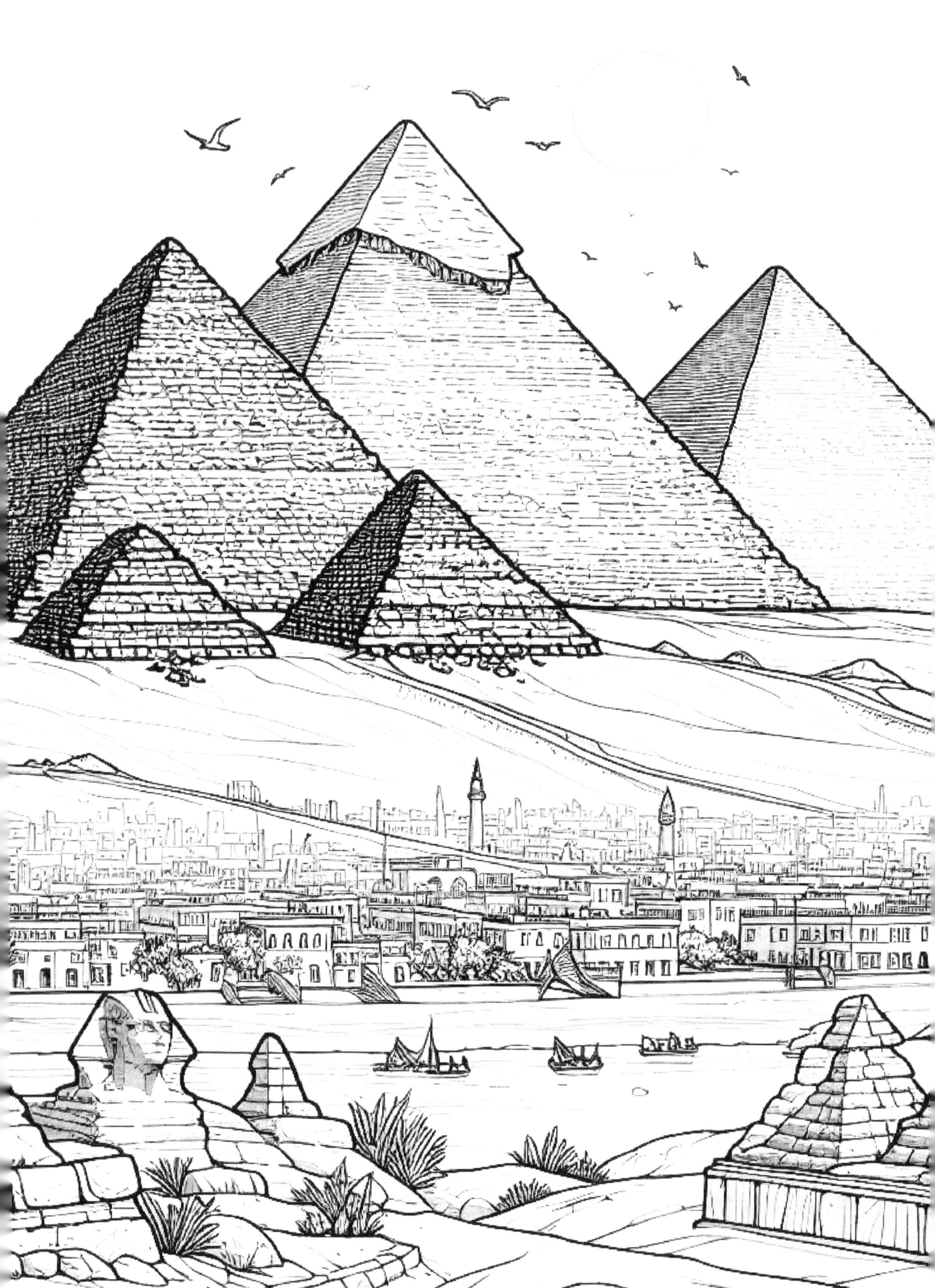

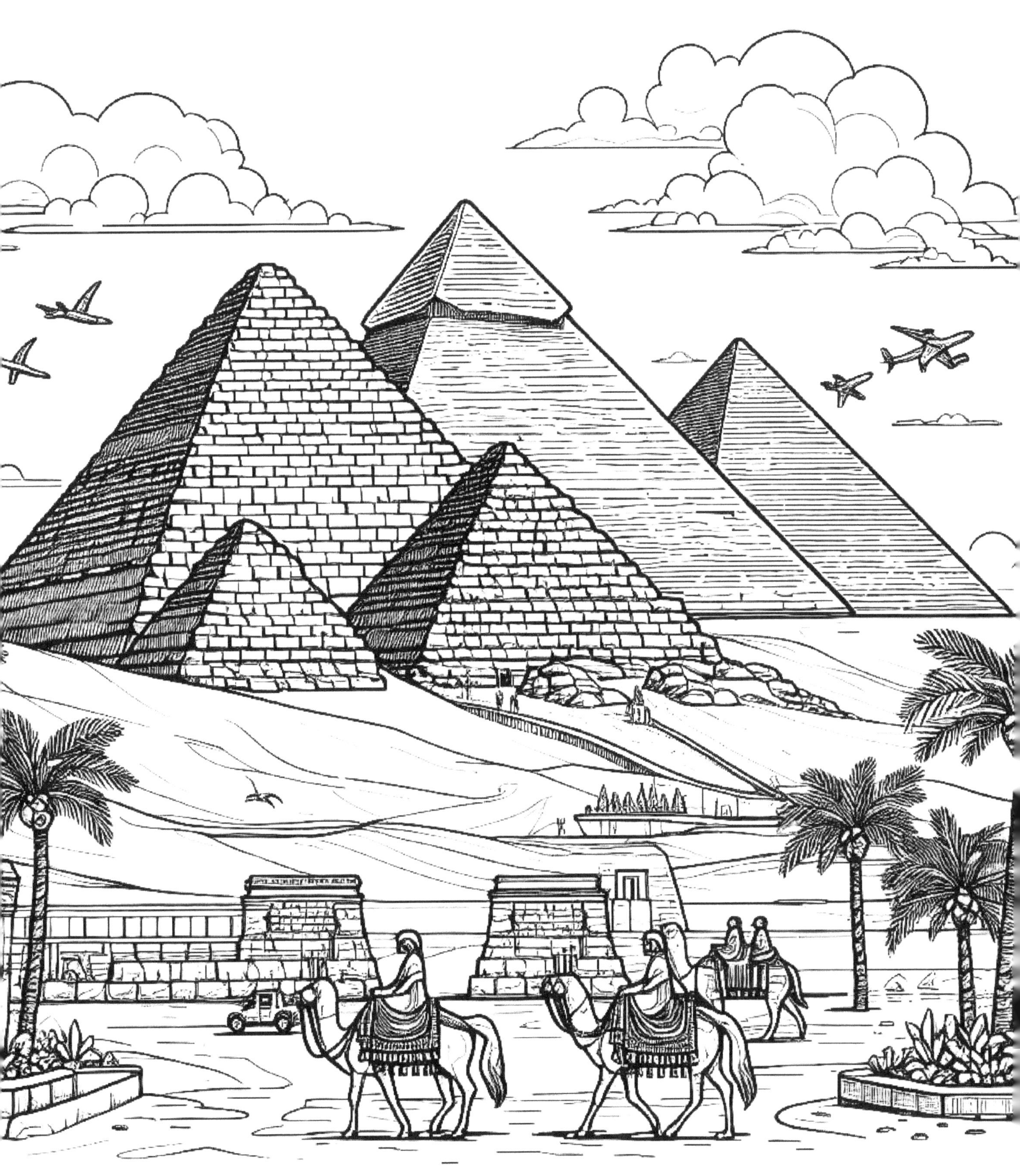

Pyramids of Giza

CAIRO, EGYPT

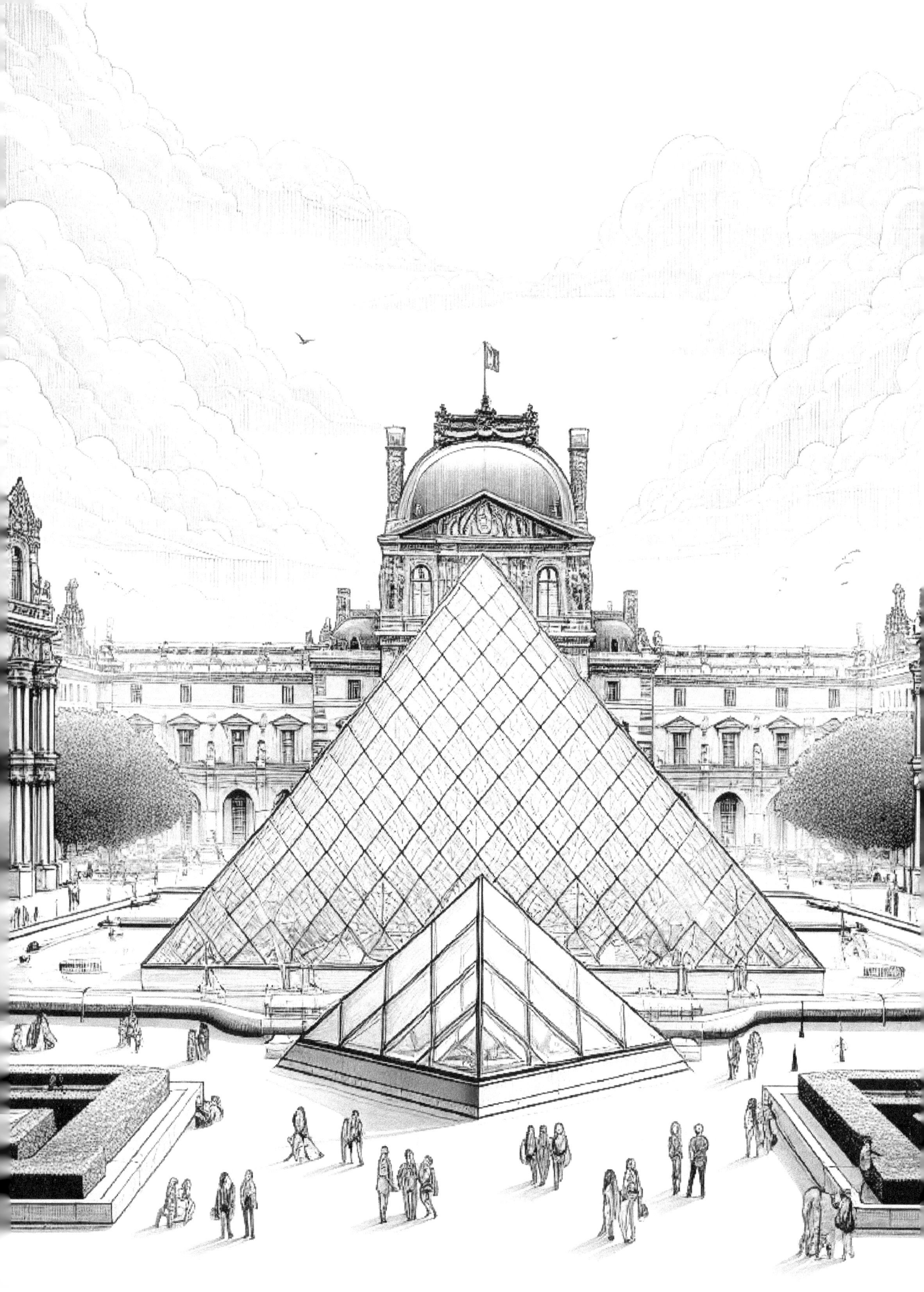

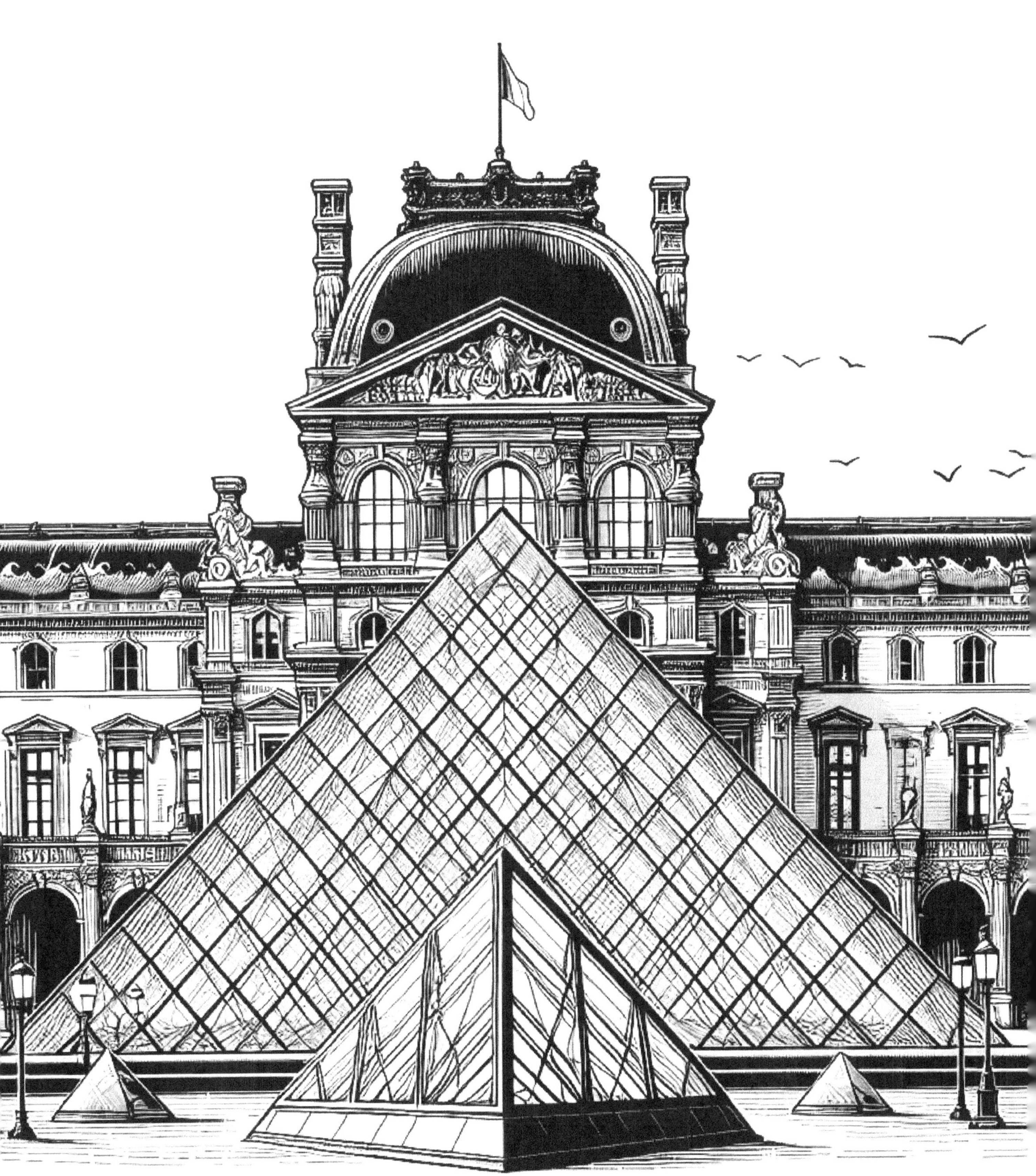

Louvre Museum

PARIS, FRANCE

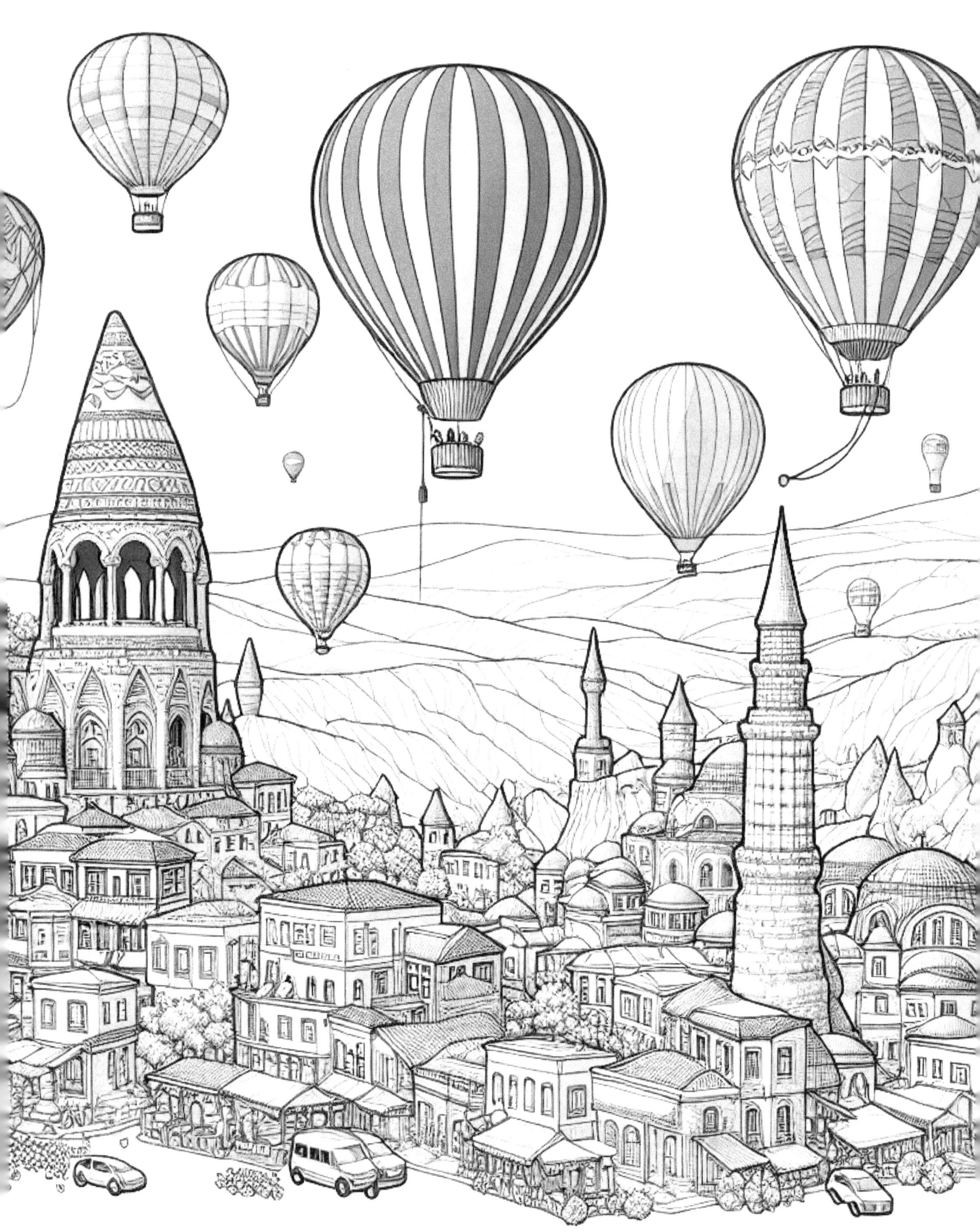

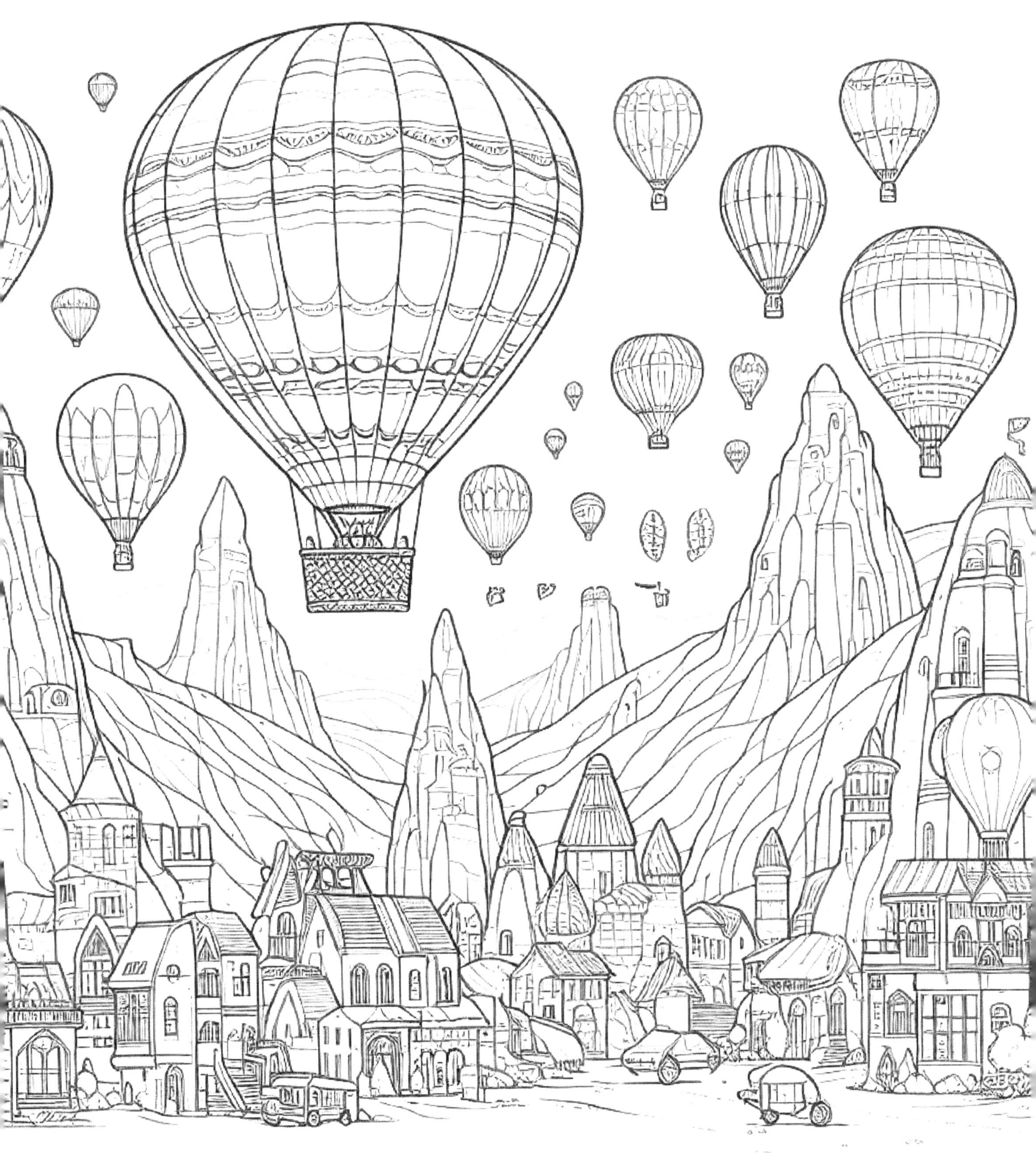

City of Balloons

CAPPADOCIA, TÜRKIYE